Occultur

"*Occulture* is one of today's most learned, unexpected, and illuminating tours through occult cultural influences. Carl Abrahamsson will expand your doors of perception of what the counterculture really is. His chapter on Anton LaVey came to me as a revelation. I am filled with hope that a book like this can be published at a time like ours."

MITCH HOROWITZ, PEN AWARD–WINNING AUTHOR OF
OCCULT AMERICA AND ONE SIMPLE IDEA

"Occulture is a word that was inevitable. During the hyperactive phase of Thee Temple Ov Psychick Youth in the 1980s we were casting around for an all-embracing term to describe an approach to combining a unique, demystified, spiritual philosophy with a fervent insistence that all life and art are indivisible. At any given moment our sensory environment is whispering to us, telling us hidden stories, revealing subliminal connections. This concealed dialogue between every level of popular cultural forms and magical conclusions is what we named 'occulture.' Carl Abrahamsson takes this rendering of an innate cultural dynamic and exposes a multitude of parallel creative Universes that do that thing. So easy to perceive with hindsight but so invisible to the closed mind, he changes our means of perception—turning a straight line into an intricate spider's web of possibilities and impossibilities combined. He performs magick; he concretizes meaning and brings forth revelation into his carefully focused vision."

GENESIS BREYER P-ORRIDGE, ENGLISH SINGER-SONGWRITER,
MUSICIAN, AND POET

"These days, too much occult discourse comes off as grandiose, needlessly arcane, or desperately darker-than-thou. But decades of participant observation on the art-magic-transgression beat have given Carl Abrahamsson a more down-to-earth approach. Streamlining Crowley, LaVey, and postpunk chaos magic, these talks and essays offer up accessible, pragmatic, and psychologically savvy takes on the intuitive potentials of creative individuation. This is not another 'system' but sparkplugs engineered for your own magical engine."

ERIK DAVIS, AUTHOR OF *NOMAD CODES: ADVENTURES IN MODERN
ESOTERICA* AND HOST OF *EXPANDING MIND* PODCAST

"A sharp, frank, and level-headed exploration of some of the most important figures and movements on the current edges of occultism. Highly recommended."

RICHARD SMOLEY, AUTHOR OF *FORBIDDEN FAITH: THE SECRET HISTORY OF GNOSTICISM*

"Carl Abrahamson's *Occulture* is itself a beautiful example of the phenomena it discusses. Erudite and a pleasure to read, the collected essays have the potential to nudge consciousness beyond the ordinary perspective of culture and history. A necessary read for students of culture or magick."

PHILIP H. FARBER, AUTHOR OF *BRAIN MAGICK, META-MAGICK,* AND *FUTURERITUAL*

"Carl Abrahamsson—that curator and champion of everything in occulture that is cool, edgy, trendy, and artsy—inspires us with this mind-expanding collection of essays: meditations on art, magick, sex, psyche, and society that collectively trace the supernatural's proclivity to cross over from counterculture to mainstream, casting light on how we see and understand our world. Not to be missed!"

RICHARD KACZYNSKI, AUTHOR OF *PERDURABO: THE LIFE OF ALEISTER CROWLEY*

"Through this collection of articles, essays, talks, and miscellanea, Carl Abrahamsson emerges as a dedicated communicator who shares concepts, histories, and ideas with insight and imagination. Whether exploring the culture of Thee Temple ov Psychick Youth or the philosophies of Crowley, Steiner, Jung, and Paul Bowles, Abrahamsson's work is never less than engaging."

JACK SARGEANT, AUTHOR OF *FLESH AND EXCESS: ON UNDERGROUND FILM, NAKED LENS: BEAT CINEMA,* AND *AGAINST CONTROL*

"A welcome collection of insightful essays on the acculturation of society from the veteran chronicler of countercultures."

HYMENAEUS BETA, FRATER SUPERIOR OF O.T.O., MUSICIAN, AND OCCULTIST

occulture

THE UNSEEN FORCES THAT DRIVE CULTURE FORWARD

Carl Abrahamsson

Park Street Press
Rochester, Vermont • Toronto, Canada

Park Street Press
One Park Street
Rochester, Vermont 05767
www.ParkStPress.com

Park Street Press is a division of Inner Traditions International

Library of Congress Cataloging-in-Publication Data

Names: Abrahamsson, Carl, author.
Title: Occulture : the unseen forces that drive culture forward / Carl
   Abrahamsson.
Description: Rochester, Vermont : Park Street Press, 2018. | Includes
   bibliographical references and index.
Identifiers: LCCN 2017025942 (print) | LCCN 2017060670 (e-book) |
   ISBN 9781620557037 (pbk.) | ISBN 9781620557044 (e-book)
Subjects: LCSH: Occultism.
Classification: LCC BF1471 .A27 2018 (print) | LCC BF1471 (e-book) |
   DDC 130—dc23
   LC record available at https://lccn.loc.gov/2017025942

Printed and bound in the United States by P. A. Hutchison Company

10 9 8 7 6 5 4 3 2 1

Text design by Virginia Scott Bowman and layout by Debbie Glogover
This book was typeset in Garamond Premier Pro with Concept Sans, Futura Std, and Avenir LT Std as display fonts

To send correspondence to the author of this book, mail a first-class letter to the author c/o Inner Traditions • Bear & Company, One Park Street, Rochester, VT 05767, and we will forward the communication, or contact the author directly at **www.carlabrahamsson.com**.

For Vanessa

Contents

★

Foreword

CARL ABRAHAMSSON, the author of the lively, engaging, and occasionally quirky writings you now hold in your hand, calls himself a "subcultural entrepreneur" whose main interest is in the strange interzone between creativity and ritual, the liminal space blending magic and art that has come to be known as occulture. What is occulture? The term is said to have been coined by the performance artist Genesis P-Orridge sometime in the 1980s and is easily recognizable as a portmanteau word combing "occult" and "culture." Abrahamsson agrees. It is a general term, he tells us, "for anything cultural but decidedly occult/spiritual."

Needless to say that covers a lot of ground. In recent years the powerful and informative links between art and the occult have become a hot topic both with artists and occultists, but anyone with some knowledge of the history of both recognizes that the association between the two predates their current popularity by some time. Hermetic ideas informed the Renaissance, and the Symbolism of the nineteenth century was rife with notions of other worlds and intimations of strange, ethereal realities. The occult interests of the Surrealists are well known, but even before them the Russian esoteric philosopher P. D. Ouspensky was inspiring Cubo-Futurist and Suprematist painters with remarks like, "In art it is necessary to study 'occultism'; the artist must be clairvoyant;

he must see that which others do not see; he must be a magician."

Yet although it has a fine pedigree reaching back perhaps into the roots of art and self-consciousness itself—the earliest known paintings, dating back some fifty thousand years, were made by our prehistoric ancestors in nearly inaccessible caves while experiencing altered states of consciousness and journeying in the spirit world—occulture is something more than an awareness that magic and art are strongly connected, notwithstanding the importance of this awareness. There is a purposive element behind the idea, a self-consciousness associated with earlier art movements, a need to define itself against the backdrop of the ever-increasing plethora of information, entertainment, and distraction that characterizes our time. Yet while many, if not most, art movements define themselves by exclusion, cutting out and rejecting everything *not* them—André Breton's banishments from the Surrealist fold are legendary—occulture works with a broader brush, embracing a wide and at times contradictory assemblage of influences and interests. In this it shares much with a movement within modern occultism with which it is often associated: chaos magick. As I understand it, in chaos magick, one need not stick to the prescribed rituals or pantheons but can make magick with just about anything, provided one's imagination is strong and one's will is in earnest. How different is this from many forms of art since Duchamp, when the touch of the artist transforms everyday items—even urinals—into mysterious portals of wonder?

The wide lens of occulture is in evidence in this brilliant collection of lectures, essays, and articles aimed, in one way or another, at conveying the peculiar aesthetic shared by its varied subjects. Where artists may have once turned up their noses at trashy occult rubbish, and occultists peered confusedly at some incomprehensible conceptual work, the occulturist is able to move easily between the two worlds. He or she is in many ways a response to serious shortfalls in either camp. Occulture rejects the blasé cynicism and self-irony that characterizes much postmodernism. It seeks in the commitment of the true magician to his practice the seriousness that has evaded art for some time now. Yet in engaging with art and wider cultural expression—film, music, fiction, theater—occulture forces the often sequestered occultist out of his magic circle and into the broader fields of creativity. Magic can be performed in the cinema, on the dance floor, and in a comic book. And art is no stranger in the halls of ritual and ceremony. In occulture these occasional fellow travelers stick together for the duration of the journey, and they usually find some very interesting places to go to.

What strikes a reader of these short, sharp forays into the occultural landscape is precisely this breadth of interest and curiosity. I get the feeling from them that their author is determined to find something fascinating in everything, to be able to, like the magician or artist, turn what we might look away from into the center of our attention. Having worked in many of the fields he writes about—producing music, film, fiction, and photography (he is a kind of Renaissance occulturist)—Abrahamsson is well equipped for his expeditions; the reader is in the hands of a good guide through a cultural terrain that is not without its pitfalls. Some of the pieces here focus tightly on magical practice, mostly of the Thelemic, that is, Crowleyan, variety, and some readers may need a bit of background in this in order to get their full import. But the main ideas are clear and seem to fit in nicely with studies of dolls, dreams, magick as a kind of "currency"—an occult Bitcoin—and the philosophy of Anton LaVey. A piece on the similarities and differences between Aleister Crowley and Rudolf Steiner draws some surprising comparisons, and one on Jung, mythology, and their appearance in contemporary culture adds some new insights to an often too-familiar theme.

My own favorites were the pieces on Paul Bowles, Ernst Jünger, and Yukio Mishima, three writers who we would not immediately consider occult, but that occulture's wide lens can easily fit into its frame. The idea of the "expat occultist," a magician constantly on the move, as it were—as Bowles seemed to have been—seems obvious, but I don't think anyone pointed it out as such before; at least I haven't seen it. Jünger and Mishima seem natural for a comparison. Both, in different ways, had a fascination with combat and battle; Jünger, of course, was a decorated war hero, while Mishima was too young to see combat, a serious failing from his point of view that troubled him throughout his short life. Both developed fastidious, highly polished prose styles. And both were, again in different ways, on the right side of the political spectrum, although Jünger's contemplative detachment is a rather different affair from Mishima's histrionic and fatal acting out.

What is important here is that Abrahamsson is taking occulture down interesting new routes, beyond the pentagrams and black leather that too often obscure its more subtle offerings and provide the uninitiated with kitschy reasons to dismiss it. He is showing that the occulturist perspective can provide new ways in which to see literature and even the act of writing itself. But what these writings do fundamentally is what all good criticism should: convey the passion and delight that the critic found in his subjects, so that the reader can share in this transformative bounty. This collection, I think, manages that admirably.

GARY LACHMAN,
LONDON, NOVEMBER 2016

GARY LACHMAN is the author of twenty books on the links between consciousness, culture, and the Western inner tradition, most recently *The Lost Knowledge of the Imagination, Beyond the Robot: The Life and Work of Colin Wilson,* and *The Secret Teachers of the Western World.* He writes for different journals in the United States, United Kingdom, and Europe, where he also lectures, and his work has been translated into several languages. He is on the adjunct faculty in Transformative Studies at the California Institute of Integral Studies. In a former life he was a member of the pop group Blondie and in 2006 was inducted into the Rock and Roll Hall of Fame. Born in New Jersey, since 1996 he has lived in London. His website is **garylachman.co.uk.**

1

Contra Contra Means Pro

Originally a lecture delivered at the Akademie der Bildenden Künste in Munich, Germany, 2015.

THE RECENT INFLUX, both in substance and attention, of magical thinking, esotericism, and spirituality in a more visible contemporary cultural context has already been well documented. This interdisciplinary lecture series* is just one example of an emergence of topics and areas that used to be banned or shunned. Why is this? I'm going to take a look at some possible explanations and shine the light on some current examples of magic, not only as a fascinating and exotic topic but as an active ingredient in contemporary cultural change.

There are so many possible definitions that I think we'll have to begin by narrowing down. Many things, developments, and changes begin in the dark, so to speak, whether it's cultural, political, business related, or interest-group related—and especially if these contain seeds or ideas that go against the current status quo. So one treads lightly, evaluates, discusses with the already initiated, and develops the change in question. That seems to be a more or less general modus operandi. We are going to stick to considerably more esoteric or occult ideas and methods this evening, meaning ideas contained within

---

*The Real Magic series that ran from 2015 to 2016. This specific lecture was followed by a conversation with Genesis Breyer P-Orridge.

1

frameworks that have traditionally been outside normal or accepted scientific or philosophical discourse and methodology.

It's complicated to look at a topic that has been so integrated in human cultural history but retrospectively mainly through fiction and myth. The reason for the vague cloudiness has usually been a mix of internal and external pressure. Esoteric groups or solitary magicians have kept teachings and techniques secret to retain an intra-group dynamic, to "protect" the teachings in question. But they have also done it because of external pressure; because it has simply been dangerous to display interest or activity within repressive cultures. Complicated codes, symbols, and initiatory structures have thereby become both fascinating and terrifying to the outsiders, who have usually been the ones to confusedly codify what they've only heard about.

One could say that the Knights Templar represented an occult counterculture. This order of military men and noblemen, active from the twelfth to the fourteenth centuries, initially supported the Catholic Church by helping pilgrims reach the Holy Land. But as they grew wealthier and also trafficked with the enemy, meaning Islam, in terms of hidden knowledge and science, the polarity increased. The Catholic Church refused competition when it came to worldly power, and this increasingly powerful group that concocted secret rituals based on enemy sources had to go. To hell, that is. After a Catholic clean sweep, complete with human sacrifice at the stake, the Templars went underground along with their mysteries, only to resurface some four hundred years later as Freemasons—according to their own myth, at least. Here we can see a continued countercultural streak, in that the Freemasonic republic of the United States disconnected from the strict Anglo-Saxon Church of England hegemony.

Strange things were going on in Germany too. The mythical Bavarian Illuminati and Rosicrucianism challenged hegemonic structures from the seventeenth century and onward, mythically empowered by occult Eastern sources and carrying an individualistic impulse that was not looked upon kindly by either church or state. There was always something going on beneath the surface but most often it was based on small secret groups interested in self-development, radical science, hedonism, or simply liberty as a principle. Some individuals from this para-occult background drifted into political movements, but many did not.

The postrevolutionary Enlightenment of the late eighteenth century stressed rationalism and empiricism, and also brought with it a slightly more liberal atmosphere. And the pendulum kept on swinging. When industrialism, the inevitable child of the Enlightenment, hit hard during the nineteenth century, the irrational yearning of Pre-Raphaelites and symbolists brought forth a bourgeois interest in altered states of consciousness, spiritualism, and Eastern philosophies. But still it was contained as specialized interests, with no real tangibility or credibility in the main cultural stream.

This changed very much during the second half of the nineteenth century, for many reasons. One main reason was that esoteric ideas and magical work became rooted in open-minded *cultural* environments rather than in insular fraternities where intra-nepotism was more important than personal development per se. The British Hermetic Order of the Golden Dawn is one of the most famous occult groups from this time. With culturally active people like William Butler Yeats, Aleister Crowley, Arthur Edward Waite, Arthur Machen, Florence Farr, and Maud Gonne the environment itself attracted individuals who wanted both sides of the coin: both an esoteric path of self-development but also techniques and strategies to use in their own creative work. The thematics of occultism spilled over into their work too, thereby helping establish a wider interest.

A parallel manifestation could be seen in the romantically Goethean world of post-Theosophy Rudolf Steiner and his Anthroposophical movement. Approaches and techniques that not long before this were regarded as mere hocus-pocus with no validity in a bourgeois society or culture now emerged as substantial parts of people's lives and creativity, and they continue being influential to this day in ecological thinking and holistic teaching methods.

However, one could argue that these were fairly soft "leaks" into the general mind frame. An exception would be Golden Dawn–trained Aleister Crowley (1875–1947). But Crowley's impact had more to do with his provocative, often scandalous personality and his need for attention rather than the core of his magical-philosophical system of Thelema, which is essentially very creative and pro-individualistic. Crowley was also interesting as someone who tried to merge a scientific attitude with inner occult research. Seeing that so much of our accepted science today has its sources within the occult sciences, Crowley's early methodological wishes may yet bring out some really radical finds. Today, it's almost as if science itself has surpassed occultism, not only in using a truly esoteric language of its own, but also in its wild speculation and research about both inner and outer space.

Considerably tougher strains of distinct counterculture popped up in slightly more expected arenas: the art world. I'm thinking specifically of Dada rather than surrealism as a post–World War One psychological safety valve. Many of the protagonists from both these scenes were interested in the then-emerging phenomena of psychology and psychoanalysis but also in more distinctly esoteric things.

André Breton's manifesto of the surrealists contains many interesting formulations:

> We must give thanks to the discoveries of Sigmund Freud. On the basis of these discoveries a current of opinion is finally forming by means of which the human explorer will be able to carry his investigation much further, authorized as he will henceforth be not to confine himself solely to the most summary realities. The imagination is perhaps on the point of reasserting itself, of reclaiming its rights. If the depths of our mind contain within it strange forces

capable of augmenting those on the surface, or of waging a victorious battle against them, there is every reason to seize them—first to seize them, then, if need be, to submit them to the control of our reason.[1]

If this is not a formulation of a magical Weltanschauung, I don't know what is. John Moffitt's book on Duchamp, *Alchemist of the Avant Garde,* also reveals many highly fascinating occult sources in the work of one of the giants of contemporary art. And there are many other examples.

One thing that's consistent in both the inspiration from and actual application of occultism is a strong sense of individualism, which may be a key ingredient in its presence in many countercultural phenomena. The history of magic shows that even when integrated in sanctioned religious or societal contexts, magical practice has been driven onward by individuals with a unique set of experimental tools. We're looking at a refinement and empowerment of the individual through a progression, symbolic and preferably real too, that will enhance not only his or her life, but also spill over in a general benevolence through wisdom. The parallels to the work of the artist are obvious.

When collective approaches are attempted, the process and results turn into something else: manipulations, politics, demagogia, power tripping, and so forth. Initial communal goals are one thing; a causal manipulation of the masses another. The history of magical groups is a history of crash landings or slow degeneration. Very seldom do we find success stories about fully developed higher creatures who spread their inner light within group contexts and beyond. Very often it's an all-too-human scenario of power struggles within groups and secret societies that pushes the potential for self-development back into the shadows in order for ego inflation and chaos to shine. This has usually brought forth a general marginalization of initially very interesting ideas. To a great extent, I believe this has to do with the use of a language and terminology that is too obfuscated, arcane, and symbolic. Instead of simply seeing what needs to be done and how, many individuals haven't been able to see the beauty of the forest because of all the trees in the way.

A sublime symbol of the swinging-pendulum phenomenon in human history is the emergence at about the same time of atomic energy and LSD. The vast potential of destruction and the vast potential of reappraisal and creation were ushered in at the same time and unleashed paranoid and fierce global power struggles on one hand and major cultural shifts on the other. I'm not saying LSD has been singularly responsible for the countercultural effects of the 1960s. But it was certainly a key agent that helped initiate a wave of major changes in the Western mind.

Integrated in the psychedelic 1960s was a major influx not only of Eastern teachings, yoga, and meditation but also of Western esotericism. The colorful open-mindedness of the times made young people question not only current political authority but also traditional authorities like the established world religions. Many people sought out magic and occultism—most in the sense of "pop occultism" and the integration of alluring symbolism, but some in a more serious and devoted way. The environment was an overall experimental one, and young people were suddenly no longer afraid to voice their own opinions.

People like Crowley, Blavatsky, and Gurdjieff became icons. Young people sought out their teachings, as the books gradually came back in print. And let's not forget Carl Gustav Jung and Hermann Hesse, who were very popular among this emerging generation, and who were both from a highly esoteric or spiritual background. This led to an integration of ideas based in the inner sphere and an empowerment that were all part of the same environment as antiwar sentiments, civil rights, women's rights, environmentalism, and many other things we take for granted today. The overall countercultural movement of the sixties unmasked various hegemonies that had been temporarily emaciated by the Second World War and its industrial atrocities. But it did so not primarily, as could be expected, by a full-frontal attack using a similar language, but rather one from various unexpected corners and in many different ways. One could say that it was like a choir of messages and resistance, but composed of individually distinct voices.

The unmasking of this perhaps unnecessary existential dualism took different forms in different media. In a general us-versus-them attitude (from both sides), even general entertainment was infused with the conflicts to a higher degree than ever before, from simple tales like the motorcycle movies *The Wild Angels* and *Easy Rider* to slightly more philosophical and paranoid examples like the wonderful British TV series *The Prisoner*. Again, a psychedelic sensibility helped change both form and content, sometimes to surprising degrees.

In literature too, the themes and forms revolved around countering the old restrictions with something new, radical, and also philosophical-magical filtered through individualism. One example could be the early literary experiments of William Burroughs and his "cut-ups" and anticontrol stances. Burroughs was very interested in magic and experimented with his own system of ritually changing things, predominantly through his literary working process.

Another illuminating example would be John Fowles's *The Magus,* from 1965, a beautiful story of an individual fighting a world of illusions based on old-school power structures and morals. This was later turned into an incredibly psychedelic film, starring Michael Caine and Antony Quinn. In a similar vein would be David Ely's 1963 novel *Seconds,* which is another intricate and ultraparanoid insight into the relationship between a frustrated individual who wants existential change but is only offered it through a highly controlled, commercial, and moralistic organization. This was also turned into a beautiful and unnerving film, starring Rock Hudson.

Many of the writers at the time were immersed not only in a

contemporary fascination with esoteric and psychological themes but also reached farther back into pagan times for philosophical inspiration. Fowles wrote,

> We often forget to what an extent the Renaissance and all its achievements sprang from a reversion to the Greek system. The relationship between paganism and freedom of thought is too well established to need any proof; and all monotheistic religions are in a sense puritan in tone—inherently tyrannical and fascistic. The great scientific triumphs of the Greeks, their logic, their democracy, their arts, all were made possible by their loose, fluid concepts of divinity; and the same is true of the most recent hundred years of human history.[2]

If we keep looking at the 1960s, another interesting countercultural angle is the creation of Anton LaVey's Church of Satan in 1966. LaVey's flamboyant, hedonistic, and life-affirming group publicly declared their hatred of the hippies and psychedelic culture, thereby affirming basic values of conservative America. But still they bore the stigma of the satanic affiliation in public opinion, thereby making them a counter-counterculture too weird and frightening to deal with.

In the early 1980s, Thee Temple Ov Psychick Youth (TOPY) was developed by British artist Genesis P-Orridge (and associates) as a social, artistic, and magical experiment. The term *occulture,* coined by P-Orridge, became not only a distanced and fascinating term but also a very active and integrated banner for individual and group behavior rooted in magic. TOPY was like a mix of a traditional magical order, a hippie commune, an active think tank developing radical ideas, and a producer of very tangible culture in terms of products like records, videos, performances, concerts, books, booklets, and many other things. The overall goal was to help the human individual to liberate herself from the chains of her past, whether psychological, emotional, sexual, cultural, religious, and so on. The biggest change, though, was that the discourse was public and nonsymbolic. One made no secret about methodology, technology, or goals. This audacity led to problems and stigmatization for the already infamous P-Orridge and eventually to the dissolution of the first phase of TOPY. But still the activities left shock waves and inspirations that carry on to this day.

The 1980s were a vital time for occultism in general. Various new branches and groups popped up in Europe and the United States, integrating new technology, psychedelics, and radical politics in work that had previously been quite academic, intellectual, and soft-spoken. This was amplified further in the 1990s, when we could see the emergence and integration of the Internet. If the magician needs a menstruum or an agent through which to send his or her desires, what better place than an invisible and far-reaching technological platform?

Although the technology of any social media platform is not countercultural in itself, the development of cryptological applications, deep webs, and other hidden (occult) platforms by definition are. One of the most interesting examples recently was the emergence of the Silk Road website, through which you could order basically anything under the radar. In a way, it represented a total and efficient individual freedom of choice using the same technology as the sanctioned market platforms. But as the market there was mainly for drugs, weapons, and other illicit items and services, it couldn't last for long. Wikileaks and other phenomena like Anonymous are similar in attitude. One uses the technology available and furthers one's own goals through a non-sanctioned development of it. The multinational IT corporations are always there with tempting and lucrative offers for the most prominent hackers.

Anonymous and also the Occupy movement's use of the masked Guy Fawkes figure from the film *V for Vendetta* reveals an esoteric connection: *V* was originally a graphic novel created by Alan Moore, whose interest in the occult is well known. Moore's integration of esoteric themes and personalities in his work has helped make several of them popular in new generations. An interesting detail is also that the film *V for Vendetta* was written by the Wachowski brothers, who had earlier created the *Matrix* trilogy—a cosmic soap opera filled not only with technological-supernatural fantasies but also imbued with a distinctly Gnostic philosophy of individual liberty. To further accentuate the contemporary malleability of a traditional outlook, the Wachowski brothers have recently morphed gender and are nowadays the Wachowski sisters.

During the autumn of 2015, some radical American occultist artists performed a public ritual and exhibition in a gallery in Los Angeles. This was in order to counter the Swiss corporation Nestlé's attempts to increase business revenues by turning water into a commodity to a greater extent than it already is. This ritual was even called a death curse and followed classic ritual methodology. It is interesting not only because of its conscious use of visibility and the provocation that brings but also because it uses magic-as-art-as-magic as an instigator for change that would normally be handled in political or intellectual arenas of protest. It isn't the objects or the art in itself here that matters, but the overall goal that these individuals hope to achieve, not by petitions and public debate, but by highly irrational yet at the same time highly structured methods.

Also recently, a Florida candidate for the Senate by the name of Augustus Sol Invictus admitted in international media that he had ritually sacrificed a goat and drunk its blood after a three-week fasting experience in the desert. No matter what will happen to Augustus I find his honesty and audacity remarkable and a very fine countercultural example of pushing the boundaries of what's accepted within "normal" society.

Femen and their bared-breasts shock tactics could be regarded in a similar way. There's nothing specifically occult about displaying your titties in protest per se, but within the specific contexts of, for instance, protests against the Vatican or fundamentalist Islam, the provocation transcends mere shock value and touches critically upon millennia-long traditions of misogynistic, antihuman, and antilife behavior.

It seems that the freer the world becomes, at least in potential, the quicker the repressive forces reply. Saudi Arabia, so prosperous in many ways, still sticks to Sharia laws and is one of the few countries in the world with an active inquisition in the form of its antisorcery squad. People are still being executed because they have been convicted of performing magic and witchcraft.

Despite isolated local draconian attitudes like this, the debate within Western academia is whether or not a "re-enchantment" is in fact taking place in our overall global culture. Religious or narrower cultic behavior signals a deep dissatisfaction with a too-rational world containing increasing threats of global annihilation as a result of short-sighted causality and hubristic empiricism. Is the emergence of thematically magical things within pop culture perhaps just the tip of the iceberg that is currently melting?

I would say that the reemergence of transcendental mind frames, sympathetic magical thinking, and ritualistic behavior fully constitutes a re-enchantment of the human psyche and of culture. The emergence of the areas and topics within academia and public visibility does not. It is interesting to note, however, that they do seem to go hand in hand. This has to a great extent been made possible by the fact that many academics and intellectuals have themselves been formatted *within* various esoteric environments like magical groups and orders in their youth. So here we see an example of how youthful experimentation can indeed lead to tangible adult presence if there is perseverance and if the time is right, so to speak. But in itself, intellectual work on the topics does not constitute a re-enchantment of our world.

Today, we can just sit back and watch very interesting goings-on. On the big level, there are things like the touring Hilma af Klint exhibition that has so far been seen by over a million people in Europe. She was hardly countercultural by definition but was clearsighted enough to realize that her work was so magical and radical, so ahead of her own times, that she stated in her will that the paintings mustn't be shown until at least twenty years after her death. Today, the time for appreciation seems more than right.

The presence of magical themes in pop culture through *Harry Potter* and *Lord of the Rings* should indicate the same thing. In a dualistic, binary, and suprarational culture, our need for mythic realms become evident and therefore violently saturated in commercial exploitation.

On a more concrete and countercultural level, we can see beautiful bookmaking as a radical tool of effecting not only change but also acting as a safeguard to preserve valuable ideas and traditions. The work of publishers like Scarlet Imprint in the UK with making exquisite editions of very radical writings, and perhaps my own work with the *Fenris Wolf* journals, are some examples of going against the grain of contemporary fragmentation and fleeting digi-culture. If ideas can create change now, that's great. But it's equally important to preserve them for future generations in lasting formats. Despite recent almost incredible technological innovations, it seems that still the two most radical innovations in human culture are the harnessing of fire and the book.

A vast amount of occulturally significant things are going on today: this lecture series, for instance, and international European Society for the Study of Western Esotericism (ESSWE) conferences within academic esotericism studies, the Here to Go symposium (biannual) in Norway, the Equinox Festival (London, 2009), the Occult Humanities Conference (New York City, 2016), the Psychoanalysis, Art and the Occult symposium (London, 2016)—a cross-fertilization between artistic and intellectual realms in real, tangible human interactions. These are not countercultural examples at all anymore, but rather evidence that what was once counter was then countered by moralistic and repressive tendencies and then eventually ended up as a constructive synthesis of beneficial ideas tangible in the real world. As in many other fields of human endeavor, it's conservative resistance to the radical resistance that makes the radical resistance strong. But if there's one thing history teaches us, sometimes painfully so, it's that life and culture are never static. The pendulum always swings.

2

Splendor Solis

Lebensreform *and Sexual Vitalism in Germany*

Originally published in the Polish magazine Trans/Wizje *(no. 6, 2015).*

THE INTERESTING AND INFLUENTIAL TRAIL of alternative lifestyles and philosophies that manifested in Germany around the turn of the nineteenth to the twentieth centuries has been well documented.* Nature-loving youth defied their heavy bourgeois programming and channeled/conceptualized a whole movement, including vegetarianism, sun worship, nudism, fasting, and an assortment of creative health cures. Some of these early protagonists moved on to America, specifically to the West Coast, and created a loose egregore that eventually gave birth to the hippies, and more.

There has always existed a long tradition of alternative thinking, as well as nature worship, in Germany. Why is that? One could of course look to the pagan past of the region as such, where Germanic tribes were defiant in the onslaught of Christian violence and propaganda. The tribal life rooted in nature wasn't unique for the Germanic sphere of course, but the strength of their resistance to change undoubtedly

---

*For instance, see Gordon Kennedy's highly recommended *Children of the Sun: A Pictorial Anthology from Germany to California 1883–1949.*

shows that they weren't willing to trade their way of life for new, strange, and arbitrary philosophies stemming from Rome and beyond.

One could easily say that one line of influence is simply tradition that eventually became mythic. The pagan past lived on, primarily in rural regions, both in stories and in the celebrations of the natural, seasonal cycles. Christians tried to revamp these cycles to fit their own ends (Christmas vis-à-vis the winter solstice would be the most obvious example), but they didn't fully succeed.

Similar challenges arose again during the Reformation. Where the hegemony of the Catholic Church had been almost total for approximately one thousand years (Sweden was the last country in Europe to be officially "christened" in 1124), Martin Luther suddenly challenged the Roman Catholic Church, and successfully so. This brought a democratization of the Christian faith and also a general sense of independence, as biblical (and other) translations into German could at this time also be distributed thanks to Gutenberg's magical printing press. Ideas and concepts were now no longer imposed from above by an authority that demanded blind faith and strict obedience. The specifically German interpretation was what mattered.

The Reformation divided the German sphere into a northeastern Protestant part and a Catholic southwestern part. Although central Europe was divided into smaller principalities, the German language and shared history brought together a form of cultural identity that in itself was strongly authoritarian—meaning you either gave orders or obeyed orders. The conservative rigidity eventually took on symbolic (as well as concrete) shape in the Prussian army and society, which was orderly and hierarchical to the extreme. When Germany was eventually turned into a single empire in 1871, the Prussian model served as an example for all these principalities.

Within this highly structured and orderly society, the exterior developments of industrialism and progress within the natural sciences brought not only material wealth but also increased pollution and waste, without forgetting increased ill health in the wake of this pollution and stress.

These parameters of progress constituted the basis for a diametrical movement—a revolt stemming from the children of the new German Reich (1871–1918). That the focus now lay on health, nature, spirituality, and so forth is hardly remarkable. That the contemporary focus on a profitable present and an almost superstitious belief in a science for the future should bring about a romantic longing for distant pagan pasts is also almost a given. A similar phenomenon can be seen in the British Pre-Raphaelite movement (ca. 1848–1870). In Germany, a yearning for an idealized state of mind and way of life became a pro-individualistic safety valve in a culture immersed in collective progress and imperialism.

Germany has always maintained an extreme psyche, in which societal and cultural developments swing from one extreme to another. Usually, one form that contains rebellion in itself can be quickly integrated within its own opposite. An example of this would be the *Wandervögel* movement (groups of free-spirited and tradition-affirming hiking boys and girls), which was quickly turned into the *Hitlerjugend* (Hitler Youth) movement after the National Socialist takeover. The Nazis had throroughly studied how the Catholic Church had gone about their business throughout the centuries, and tried to integrate similar "adaptations." Their inclusion of runic symbolism, a longing for past glories (German ones only, of course), solar worship, and so on all stemmed from late-nineteenth-century *Lebensreform* movement(s). With these attractive elements heavily flaunted in their demonstration of power, plus the integration of the blind faith of Catholicism, the Prussian model of organization, a great demagogue in Hitler, and assorted scapegoating patterns to boot, the Nazi success was swift and efficient.

The generation born in Germany in the late nineteenth century was fed up with what was being offered. What better way to protest than to just head out into nature in a highly romanticized state of mind? They also soon found out that there had already been precursors in older generations who had explored exciting phenomena like nudism and vegetarianism.

Gusto Gräser (1879–1958), a young freethinker and nomad from Austria, had been in touch with *Lebensreform* protagonists Richard Ungewitter (1869–1958) and Karl Wilhem Diefenbach (1851–1913). These meetings contributed to Gräser's formulating ideas about a colony in nature, where free love and healthy vegetarian diets could rule supreme. The Monte Verita community, established by Henri Oedenkoven and Ida Hofmann in 1900 at Ascona in Switzerland, soon became a melting pot for alternative lifestyles and attracted creative people from all of Europe (Hermann Hesse, Carl Jung, Isadora Duncan, and D. H. Lawrence, to mention but a few). Gusto Gräser became a sort of wanderer-poet in residence and attracted a lot of starry-eyed visitors. Monte Verita became like a magnet for the curious and open-minded, and also a generator for many spin-off ideas.

The concepts permeating Monte Verita were a condensed mix that were part of the greater movement called *Lebensreform:* a reformation of how life should be led, away from the big cities and the waste of aggressive capitalism. One could say that the ideas were old (perhaps even mythic) and had been filtered for some time through a general German health consciousness up until this critical era when a young generation of Germans simply started acting out rather than just talking about change. It's interesting to see how even basic concepts like hiking in nature became politicized in the Germanic sphere. The original *Naturmenschen,* like those at Ascona, simply wanted to be free and to experiment, roaming the forests and hills. The Nazis immediately wanted to wipe off any kind of romanticism involved and focus on strenghtening young boys' and girls' sense of collective belonging (the perfect platform for propaganda). The also-present Socialist stress on hiking focused on the health of the new class of industrial workers. So, no matter which perspective, German nature was the stage of political agendas as well as of necessary reflection and soul searching for the entire nation.

The artist most frequently associated with the *Lebensreform* movement, "Fidus" (Hugo Höppener, 1868–1948), painted rituals and idyllic frolicking in the sunshine, with nude men, women, and children. The images were often adorned with runic or pseudo-runic letters, to tie in the fantasies to a glorious past of pastoral pagan bliss. Solar worship is almost always prominent in his images. The idealized iconography of Fidus's paintings often borders on cartoonish kitsch that brings to mind the later Nazi propaganda of *Körperkultur* (body culture). But seen in its own temporal context, Fidus's art comes across as romantically idealistic.

On a more structured level, interesting things were going on parallel to this in German para-Masonry. The Ordo Templi Orientis, founded and run by Austrian paper industrialist Carl Kellner (1851–1905) and Theodor Reuss (1855–1923), integrated mysteries from the East, including sexual rituals for the highest degrees. The influx came from Indian tantrism and was then developed further as British occultist Aleister Crowley (1875–1947) got involved. The merging of Crowley's own religious text *Liber AL vel Legis* (*The Book of the Law*) with the structure of the OTO created a perfect vehicle for what he defined as a "solar-phallic" initiatory system. Reuss incidentally (or not) established an OTO presence at Monte Verita by, among other things, reviving the Hermetic Brotherhood of Light (a mystical order working with sex magic) and arranging a conference there in 1917, which contained a reading of Crowley's Gnostic Mass: his dramatic public celebration of solar-phallicism and the creativity of Eros.

Where most of the individuals involved were regarded as freaks or morally degenerate, some people managed to break the general ice. Pioneers like Louis Kuhne (1835–1901), Benedict Lust (1872–1945), and Adolf Just (1859–1936) wrote books about their health-reform ideas that became bestsellers, with worldwide translations to follow. This in itself contributed to a similar wave of radical health thinking in America. Rudolf Steiner created his Anthroposophic movement out of his own disappointment with Theosophy. He managed to convince thousands of people—including quite a few wealthy ones—that a new and occult way of looking at the world was totally possible to integrate in an otherwise normal lifestyle and outlook. Soon there was an impressive study center outside of Basel (the Goetheanum), newly formed Waldorf schools, teachings on how to farm more consciously and grow organic vegetables (the origins of biodynamic farming), and so on. Steiner was an enthusiastic and creative pioneer who inspired others by synthesizing and rephrasing previously too-radical concepts and making them understandable for common people. Where Monte Verita was an inspiration for curious outcasts and artists, Anthroposophy became more of an integrated movement with a potential for substantial change.

Not surprisingly, Steiner's cosmology contained many insights into the relationship between Sun and Earth, between the human spirit and body:

> We must transform ourselves, through the light, into beings who no longer experience their connection with the Earth, but feel connected to the cosmic spaces. Gradually, the contemplation of the stars, the Sun, the Moon, and cosmic space must become as familiar to us as plants growing in the meadow. If we are merely children of the Earth, we look down upon the plants covering the meadow. We enjoy them, but we don't understand them, for we remain earthly beings weighed down by gravity. As earthly beings bound by gravity, we have learned to stand on the Earth. But if we could transform ourselves, we could connect ourselves with the widths of cosmic space—those meadows of the heavens, seeded with stars.[1]

Steiner had been researching Johann Wolfgang von Goethe (1749–1832) at university, and there's really no way of escaping this master when looking at *anything* German. Goethe's anti-Catholicism and pro-sexual attitudes, and not forgetting his reverence for nature as such, made him the ideal symbol for the more intellectually inclined *Lebensreform* people. Steiner wrote that "Goethe was filled with this yearning when he wrote his essay on the *Metamorphosis of Plants*. Many of his statements were those a person would make who felt oriented to the Sun rather than the Earth—a person who felt that the Sun pulls the force of the plant's growth out of the Earth while it is still hidden underground."[2]

A typical phenomenon at the time was also a reformation of the view of the body in art and creative expression. Although there was nude revelry and dancing at Monte Verita, the most striking photographs are those from dance performances arranged by Rudolf von Laban. Photographs of elegant human bodies clothed in free-flowing and strongly colored light robes still make an impression. They remind one of Rudolf Steiner's system of physical expression: eurythmics. The spiritual and semantic gestures and poses made by colorful robe-clad dancers move the communication from the intellect to the human body as such.

As we all know, things quickly changed when the National Socialists came to power. The healthy outdoors Sun gave way for the mystical Black Sun; the *Wandervögel* became *Hitlerjugend;* fertility cults became baby factories, complete with *Mutterkreuz* (mother's cross) medals (after eight German babies had been produced by the same mother); pagan sites of worship became centers for political demagogy; and so forth. Using the Christian-Catholic method of appropriation, Goebbels, Himmler, and company scouted the lay of the land and used what they found applicable to the chaotic German mind frame. The individual was sacrificed for the collective, and yet many healthy elements remained. The problem was that everything needed to be prefixed with *German, National Socialist,* or *Hitler*—which of course excluded everyone and everything else.

One should note too that many of the protagonists that inspired the Monte Verita activities were as steeped in Ariosophy and racial theories as many of their purely political contemporaries. Richard Ungewitter, although radical in his nudism and vegetarianism, was a devout anti-Semite and associated with one of the publications favored by Adolf Hitler early on: *Ostara*. However, when the Nazis came to power, vegetarianism could be condoned (the most famous vegetarian being of course Hitler himself) but not nudism. Ungewitter remained respected in some ways but was not allowed to be outspoken about his interests. Heinrich Pudor's nudism was even more adamantly tied in to racial theories, but his criticism of the decadent laxness(!) of the Nazis naturally created a problematic situation for him.

The clearest example of how *Lebensreform* permeated even the most conservative environments in Germany is probably the physical educator Hans Surén. As a commander at the army's School for Physical Exercise, he introduced things like mud baths and nude cross-country running for the cadets. Although politically aligned with the National Socialists, his ideas were simply deemed too extreme, and the cadets eventually had to get dressed in new and swastika-adorned uniforms.[3]

In socialist circles too, nudism was integrated in a political scheme, as has been pointed out by scholar John Alexander Williams: "Like social hygiene, sex reform was a normative ideology that called on workers to transform themselves into more rational and disciplined human beings. Together, social hygiene, sex reform, and anticapitalism were all founts of socialist nudist ideology—a set of intertwined influences that distinguished this branch of nudism from the nonsocialist branch."[4] Permeating most of these characters and groups, loose or tight, was the explicit core need to return to nature and embrace the sun, symbolically in temples and concretely in exterior nature. The question then emerges: Why all of this solar and alternative force in the Germanic sphere?

It is interesting to note how the sun is a feminine noun in German: *die* Sonne. With the moon being masculine (*der* Mond), we see a distinct and early difference from the Latin and its later variants (French, Spanish, Italian, etc.), in which the sexual connotations are reversed. In a cultural sphere where the sun is suddenly a feminine, maternal energy and the nocturnal moon a paternal energy, one could draw some speculative conclusions: giving life and survival is associated with fire, light, and heat, whereas paternal protection and strength come from a sphere of darkness and cold, reflected in a pale, poetic moon. Where the Hindu solar symbol, the swastika, gives the visual impression of spinning deasil (with the sun, or clockwise), the National Socialist–Ariosophic variant spins widdershins (against the sun). This was carefully constructed to make an impression in the outer world and perhaps even on magical levels. The uniforms and insignia of the SS, black and with shiny metal death's-heads, connote a shadow world rather than the otherwise so heavily promoted healthy living of solar "children" playing in nature without apparent order.

Another interesting psychological trait is that Germans call their country *Der Vaterland* (the Fatherland), whereas most other nations tend to regard their nation as a mother or as feminine (as in Mother Russia, for instance, or *la* France).

Many ancient fertility rites in the old German regions contained fire and solar symbols. Midsummer and other seasonal peaks were celebrated with bonfires, and many obejcts (as well as living beings) related to sowing or harvesting were concretely sacrificed in holy oak-fueled fire.

J. G. Frazer recounts several fascinating and sexualized old customs in medieval Germany in his classic study *The Golden Bough:*

> At nightfall the whole male population, men and boys, mustered on the top of the hill; the women and girls were not allowed to join them, but had to take up their position at a certain spring half-way down the slope. On the summit stood a huge wheel completely encased in some of the straw which had been jointly

contributed by the villagers; the rest of the straw was made into torches. From each side of the wheel the axle-tree projected about three feet, thus furnishing handles to the lads who were to guide it in its desecent. The mayor of the neighbouring town of Sierck, who always received a basket of cherries for his services, gave the signal; a lighted torch was applied to the wheel, and as it burst into flame, two young fellows, strong-limbed and swift of foot, seized the handles and began running with it down the slope. A great shout went up. Every man and boy waved a blazing torch in the air, and took care to keep it alight so long as the wheel was trundling down the hill. The great object of the young men who guided the wheel was to plunge it blazing into the water of the Moselle. . . . As it rolled past the women and girls at the spring, they raised cries of joy which were answered by the men on the top of the mountain; and the shouts were echoed by the inhabitants on the opposite bank of the Moselle.[5]

With the Nazi *Machtübernahme* (takeover), human sexuality was again restrained after a period of considerable freedom. The Third Reich brought functionalism and purpose back to sex. Women became lauded breeding machines for racially superior children (future soldiers, no doubt). The cult of the athletic body was maintained to quite a great extent but always demagogically so. Free love was now literally a thing of the past. Although Monte Verita had already passed its peak by 1933, the people still residing there must surely have felt lucky that Ascona was in Switzerland and not in Germany. The Swiss Anthroposophists must have felt the same way. In Germany proper, Anthroposophy was duly banned after the Nazi takeover.

During the first two decades of the twentieth century, there were basically two radical movements in the Germanic sphere: one mental/intellectual and one intuitive/corporeal. Psychoanalysis, modernism,

Dada, and a conscious, political discourse are examples of the first strain; *Lebensreform* is the prime example of the second strain. Seemingly, the strains were kept apart. Perhaps they were regarded by everyone involved as incongruous? Had someone been able to merge the two, truly radical things could have happened. The greatest success story of the time, and also the person whose philosophy carried the greatest potential for merging the two, Rudolf Steiner, was in every way spiritual-corporeal rather than intellectual-corporeal.

In many ways one could argue that the National Socialists did indeed manage to combine the two strains successfully: intellectual *and* corporeal. The problem was that their concept as such came at a very high price: restricted individual liberty, the Second World War, and mass human sacrifice. And, let's not forget it, a totally devastated and fire-soaked Vaterland.

The later concept of the "Black Sun" and its esoteric mysteries within a post-Nazi mythos is highly interesting in this regard. It's an almost perfect symbol of the dark side of a culture and history so utterly steeped in different facets of solar worship. Nicholas Goodrick-Clarke's *Black Sun* is a fascinating introduction to this vast area of research:

> As in the case of the Ariosophists in the early twentieth century, political isolation in a hostile world committed to liberalism has led many neo-Nazi and neo-fascist groups to embrace occult notions of ancient Aryan wisdom. From the 1970s onward, right-wing extremists began to repackage the old ideology of Aryan racism, elitism and force in new cultic guises involving esotericism and Eastern religions. In Austria and Germany, the former SS man Wilhelm Landig revived the ariosophical mythology of Thule, the supposed polar homeland of the ancient Aryans. He coined the idea of the Black Sun, a substitute swastika and mystical source of energy capable of regenerating the Aryan race.[6]

At the bottom of the main dilemma lies perhaps not only the sun as a symbol of fiery and pagan motherly energies but also the more human aspect of life force in Eros. Central to the *Lebensreform* ideas was a breach with monogamic behavior patterns. If everyone was in the nude and healthy, not only was there a "democratization" of sorts but also an underlying (or overt) sexual energy present. This, of course, created tangible challenges in environments like Monte Verita, as among smaller communities of "amateur" naturists and nudists. It's not surprising that family was militantly stressed by both sides during the Weimar Republic that followed after the First World War. The socialists wanted to create family units of a healthy working class and the National Socialists wanted the same, with racial motives on top.

The eroticism of the *Lebensrefom* movement was always deeply rooted in nature and in rurally based fantasies about individual attraction and begetting new, sun-drenched life. In many ways, they were perhaps correct in their anti-urban assumptions. The urban sexuality of early twentieth-century Germany seemed either debauched and neurotic, as in the almost clichéd depictions of Weimar decadence in Berlin, or carefully constructed and controlled via the Nazis' eugenic visions of purity.

Lebensreform's moral breach with the oppressive Christian cult(ure), and their focus on the human body in nature (naked or not), vitalizing food, abstinence from alcohol and tobacco, as well as a romantic yearning for pagan days, basically sexualized an entire generation. As many of these overall themes already existed in German culture, it was the sexual freedom that became the most radical aspect of this cocktail. Regardless if it was made manifest in modernist art, intellectual theories, pre-hippie-esque "free love," or as specialized magico-sexual techniques within the OTO and similar fraternities, the extreme individualization of sex was the singular greatest threat to any homogenized "Germanicism." The free-flowing energy of love was therefore the first victim as Eros drifted into Thanatos in not only National Socialist theory and practice but also in its rich and powerful iconography. The young soliders-to-be of the *Hitlerjugend,* and the blond-braided beauties of the *Mädel-bünde* (maidens league) were of course not encouraged to explore each other to reach cosmic insights and unions of love, but simply to become obedient breeders of racially pure Aryans.

In August of 1903, an article on the goings-on in Ascona was published in a San Francisco newspaper, followed by many more. Some key people in the German movement emigrated to America at about the same time. Perhaps the most important character was William "Bill" Pester (1886–1963), born in Saxony but from 1906 and onward settled in California, where he lived as a "nature boy" (immortalized by fellow naturalist eden ahbez in his song of the same name, "Nature Boy," which was turned into a smash hit by Nat "King" Cole).

The wisdom of the German and German-influenced nature boys, through newspaper articles and radio broadcasts, influenced an American generation that was to bloom fully during the 1960s: the hippies. Hermann Hesse's novels *Steppenwolf* and *Siddhartha,* steeped in concepts that he had integrated while visiting Monte Verita, became huge influences on this budding generation of American freethinkers. It would probably be a simplification to say that the earlier beatniks could fit the mold too. The beats were far too self-indulgent in their own explorations of altered states of consciousness and life as a journey, come what may. It was the hippies who not only wanted to return to nature in peace, but also actively integrated many of the *Lebensreform* ingredients: free love, vegetarianism, nudism to varying degrees, and so forth. It's no wonder that this imported kind of pagan solar worship caught on in sunny California.

This movement created a foundation for what we can see around us today in the Western sphere: ecological awareness, organic and biodynamic farming, holistic perspectives within a dynamic and open-minded spirituality, and an integrated liberal sexuality. Although totalitarian systems around the world tried to appropriate the key elements from the *Lebensreform* movement, it seems the elements still work best underneath the umbrella of individual liberty and under the naked benediction of the sun.

3

Abstraction Made Concrete

The Occultural Methods and Mutations of Thee Temple Ov Psychick Youth

Originally a lecture delivered at Nekropolis Bogcafé in Copenhagen, Denmark, 2013.

I AM HERE TODAY to talk about an interesting phenomenon that existed for approximately ten years, between 1982 and 1992. This phenomenon was like a mix between a magical order, a think tank, an archive, an experiment in intentional art, and many other things. I'm talking about Thee Temple Ov Psychick Youth, or TOPY for short, which spread out of the UK and into the world and soon reached thousands of members and/or subscribers to TOPY's frequent newsletters and information.

My own involvement in this began around 1984, when I started out as a humble subscriber to newsletters and bought records, pamphlets, fanzines, and so forth, from TOPY's own mail-order service in the United Kingdom. I was very interested in all things occult at the time, and I immediately realized that TOPY was something brand-new. Everything I had read about magic and occultism always dealt with something old, arcane, systematically symbolic, and quite dusty. But not so with TOPY. I was enthused and got involved. I started working with the UK people and set up a Scandinavian branch or "access point," aptly called TOPYSCAN. This later developed into TOPYEUROPE, which for me meant basically a lot of administration run out of my little apartment in Stockholm.

It was an incredibly creative time, I have to say. TOPYSCAN, TOPYEUROPE, and an affiliated company I started called Psychick Release put out books, cassettes, CDs, vinyl records, and videocassettes and arranged workshops, lectures, film and video screenings, concerts as well as more esoteric things like group rituals and magical workshops for those really active within this highly pragmatic sphere.

Some time in 1991 I burned out and decided to not carry on, as the adminsitration had simply become so overwhelming. Interestingly enough, the key people in the United Kingdom and the United States had felt exactly the same thing at about the same time. We basically decided it was time to end TOPY as we knew it. A first phase of ten hyper-interesting years had gone by.

So where do we begin when looking at this phenomenon? If we look to the United Kingdom, we can recognize some well-known people. Artist Genesis P-Orridge and his collaborators at the time (like Peter Christopherson from the former project Throbbing Gristle, and David Tibet, an Aleister Crowley romantic who also formed the band Current 93) decided to try to create a group synthesizing their own inspirations in art and magic and at the same time commenting upon or influencing the harsh political climate of the United Kingdom.

With magical mentors like Aleister Crowley, Austin Osman Spare, tribal shamanism, and the literary and artistic cut-up applications of William Burroughs and Brion Gysin, and artistic seeds like the surrealists, Dada, mail art, situationism, sixties counterculture, and many, many other things, a core developed that would grow to form Thee Temple Ov Psychick Youth as a communal and quaquaversal entity rather than a hierarchic traditonal order with followers.

At center stage of this new hybrid was a video group that also made music, called Psychic Television, or PTV. This was formed by P-Orridge, Christopherson, and musician Alex Fergusson, and David Tibet was in there too at an early stage. Taking advantage of the unlikely successes and infamy of the predecessor Throbbing Gristle, the group secured record deals with major labels like Warner and CBS, which at the time was almost beyond fluke level. But it happened. PTV started recording music and making videos that soon became a very integrated part of TOPY and its philosophy.

There was a great deal of writing going on too, with the most well-known text being *Thee Grey Book*. What was it all about? What was the actual philosophy of TOPY? Well, it's clear to see that there was a great deal in it of Crowleyan Thelema—that is, of Crowley's philosophy of will and considerate subjectivism. But there was an amplification of this more general attitude of "Do what thou wilt" in the technical sorcery system of British painter and magician Austin Osman Spare and the cut-up methodology of writer William Burroughs and painter Brion Gysin—all latter-day TOPY saints of course. The core was one of sacralized free will, and an experimental technology was presented to root out bad habits, whether imposed by others or simply one's own, and generate change through, quite often, artistic means.

PTV was very productive, and also worked with other filmmakers like Derek Jarman, John Maybury, and Cerith Wyn Evans, to create a cinematic or televisual corpus of ritual footage, poetic propaganda, and psychedelic playfulness. The musical side of things took the entourage on the road to many, many concerts all over the world. An example of this first phase could be my own first experience of PTV live, which was in Stockholm in 1984. There was one video screening of their material at Konstfack, a college of art, on the first night and then a regular concert (which also included the videos) at a rock club on the following night. There was a presence in both worlds, so to speak.

TOPY was not a hierarchical group or order. This was interesting, as most of esoteric history comes out of very hierchical fraternities. It's more correct to say that TOPY was a meritocracy structured atomically. The proton would be a "station" or an "access point"—that is, local points in time and space—and around these members and interested people constituted electrons and simply revolved.

One key magical technique that mixed transformative potential with artistic expression was the process called sigilization. Formulated well by Austin Spare in his books, it basically meant stripping the conscious formulation of your desired goal into smaller particles or denominators that could then be creatively readjusted into new and highly un- or subconscious forms during some form of ecstatic mind frame—most often of a sexual kind. This should be done in an as aestheticized way as possible, for instance on a sheet of paper, and also include sexual liquids, blood, and hair. This would then constitute one's own very private and vividly symbolic manifestation of will.

According to TOPY's integration of William Burroughs's mind-boggling romanticism concerning the number 23, this sigilizing ritual should be performed on the 23rd of each month at 2300 hours. If you began that process, you were given a Temple name: "Eden" and a number for men, and "Kali" and a number for women. If you completed 23 such sigils, you became elevated, not necessarily in rank but certainly in respect. But it was also totally possible to keep this process a secret if you so desired.

These special sigils were sent in to the TOPY stations (United Kingdom, United States, and eventually Europe), where they were filed in confidence. I don't think there has ever existed such a unique collection of heterogeneous yet philosophically resonant magical art.

This technique was the central one for active TOPY members. But there were also other rituals that were performed together, quite often for communal goals and projects, but sometimes also for greater altruistic purposes; these were very often sexual in nature and method but not all the time. In the UK and United States, workshops were held with a Native American Indian shaman called Nomad, and in

Scandinavia we did similar things with the Norwegian shaman Arthur Sørensen and also with the percussionist and wizard-artist z'ev. This was focused on a more classical form of shamanism, with mind travels to the different spheres or "worlds" and communications with what- or whoever was found there.

Another overall method was filtering or stripping thoughts and sentiments from the past, so they could fit our contemporary times. Promoting forgotten geniuses like Spare, beat iconoclasts like Burroughs or poet Harry Crosby, to mention but a few, catapulted these spirits into the psyches of a generation brought up on despair and desolation. These pioneers had shown that it was possible, like Crowley had prophesied, to "do what thou wilt," but certain psychic barriers had to be torn down or deconstructed first. TOPY helped administer some of these tearing-down techniques.

There were other magical groups of like mind around at the time. The Illuminates of Thanatheros (IOT) generated a vortex of what they called chaos magic, with a similar hardcore and pragmatic approach, often ingrained with scientific terms of the day, such as from quantum physics. The Order of the Nine Angles (ONA) was a more sinister and dark group or, rather, collective, of individuals exploring Satanic motives and motivations. It is interesting to see that stagnant fraternal, traditional orders dealing with some kind of esoteric teaching or practical magic, and a political climate that was based in a fiercely conservative approach to handling things (à la Margaret Thatcher's government) actually became fertile soil for truly thinking out of the box. TOPY was never interested in politics per se, but activley promoted individual liberty on all levels and also fought for some pragmatic goals such as then-current wildlife or animal rights issues.

As this entire environment was deeply rooted in a postpunk or do-it-yourself (DIY) culture, the emphasis on a "cottage industry" psychology turned into great signal and very little noise. Almost every TOPY station or access point had its own setup for producing printed matter, records, videos, and so on, all talismanic and carrying a magical charge in their own peculiar way. Even if only for internal distribution, the output was big and local distribution warmly taken care of by devoted members.

Hence the concept of occulture saw the light of day, as hundreds of TOPY members digested and divested arcane lore in new and pop-scientific ways to a DIY generation frustrated with lies, blunt propaganda, and mass-market ersatz commodities. From the glamorous spheres of occultism and counterculture, there now emerged occulture, containing sharp philosophies, magical technologies, kudos to those who had worked before us—whether in art or magic—and a general sense of enthusiasm in reveling in the great mystery of life and existence. TOPY made out-of-print books available in photocopies to members, and forgotten musics were widely disseminated via cassette tapes. Ditto for forgotten yet inspiring films on VHS cassettes and pirate broadcasts. A lot of previously impossible-to-find things were suddenly made available.

This essential theme of availability became bedrock, an essential foundation. Pragmatically appropriating and recontextualizing hidden morsels of subversive seed (and flowers) soon became a practical method, in which previous levels of abstraction—not seldom placed there because of the need for self-preservation—became very concrete indeed. It was almost as if the process evolved smoother and faster exponentially—meaning, the more, the merrier.

That's one level of concretization: demystifying old codes, and spelling them out in an attitude of inquisitive analysis—"Can we use this for something?" This was true within TOPY not only in breaking symbolic codes in traditional occultism and hermeticism but also in pop-cultural appropriations. An example: Burroughs and Gysin were demigods in the TOPY mythology. Lots of literature was available, but there was more to it. Genesis managed to borrow 16 mm prints of the legendary Antony Balch films with Burroughs and Gysin from the 1960s. I then traveled with these prints and showed them in Berlin and other places at independent cinemas, thereby not only reverently resonating with our icons, but also spreading them in a wider, cultural context. I also traveled with a film program called "Visions of Occulture" in 1989, which had Benjamin Christensen's beautiful film *Häxan* (the *Witchcraft through the Ages* version, narrated by William Burroughs) and some Jodorowsky films. The same was true here: intraorder mythology and pop-cultural expressions in a wider context—and at the same time.

Psychick Release also republished some out-of-print books about runes in Swedish by older scholars. This was relevant to our own availability in terms of the material. Rare book and manuscripts appeared, new contacts were made, and many opportunities arose. This generated a field of dynamic creativity, in which many, many synchronicities appeared and greased the machine further.

When the first TOPY phase ended something else immediately began. The Internet began, and with this a paradigm shift unparalleled in the history of human civilization. Immediately there emerged a fiction-based subculture called cyberpunk in which strains of the TOPY inspirations Burroughs, J. G. Ballard, and Philip K. Dick were established even more prominently than during the 1980s, when it was mainly singular key people like P-Orridge and Joy Division singer Ian Curtis who brought attention to important instigators like this.

A new cyberpunk culture emerged that both feared and loved the Internet. Magazines like the American *Mondo 2000* questioned, codified, defined, and redefined culture in Internet times. One prime mover in the shadows was, again, Genesis P-Orridge, who had been exiled to California after the demise of TOPY in 1991–92. As a result of those early cyber movements came the successful *Matrix* films, after which followed a massive infusion of general hocus-pocus in film and in literature: *Lord of the Rings, Harry Potter, Twilight,* and so on. Bland mass-market expressions, yes, but still probably very indicative of a world in need of some serious re-enchantment. Especially if we consider the enormous successes of all these films and franchises.

Schematically, the Internet is basically carrying on in a TOPY tradition, whether conscious of it or not: making things available, empowering an exchange of ideas and thoughts, promoting human development, encouraging pioneering piracy rather than stale complacency—perhaps in some ways infringing, but in the hope that some kind of good mutation would happen because of it.

A term like *occulture* is today widely used both within academia and in pop writing. Basically signifying the same thing as when P-Orridge coined the term: the sphere of impact in general society of building blocks or "memes" previously kept hidden for various reasons and thereby becoming glamorous enough to draw attention to themselves. Occulture is also when a previously occulted behavioral pattern or technique for effecting change in accordance with will is integrated in general society and accepted as reasonable behavior. The past decades' wave of pop yoga and pop meditation could be seen as examples of this.

In 2009, a volume called *Thee Psychick Bible* was published by Feral House.[1] The first edition also came with a DVD, with a selection of some of the early TOPY films. The book proper contains basically all documents and writings that were official TOPY teachings. What was surprising was not that most of it had matured quite nicely and wasn't as dated as I think many old-timers had suspected. The most surprising thing was the interest in the market, so to speak. The first edition sold out, and a paperback version has been out since then, selling thousands of copies. This should indicate that there's a respect for the TOPY phenomenon as such and that the ideas presented back then are equally valid today—if not even more so.

Psychic TV is still around, touring, making music and videos, predominantly as a psychedelic rock group called Psychic TV3. And I'm currently here in Copenhagen to show a film based on or inspired by

PTV's seminal 1983 album *Dreams Less Sweet*. I think it was American Apparel that earlier this year released a T-shirt with the "psychick cross," a logo trademarked by P-Orridge. That was quickly removed. But it's still interesting that in the psyches of these industrial hipster designers this symbol somehow exists and feeds back something quite substantial, regardless of whether they're conscious of it or not.

Another interesting phenomenon today is of course the massive interest both within the art world and academia for predominantly Western esotericism. I'm not saying TOPY alone can take a bow for this, but, ending twenty-three years ago, there had certainly been a full decade's worth of bringing out exactly that: artists dealing with topics spiritual, iconoclastic, or both. The recent exhibition of Hilma af Klint's paintings has so far been seen by over a millon people. The Venice Biennale of 2013 was immersed in art and spirituality, displaying not only Jung's *Red Book* but also Frieda Harris's Crowley-designed Thoth Tarot paintings. In younger generations of artists, esoteric themes overflow, and when they backtrack in the more recent history of magic and esoteric art, they will surely find TOPY material or formulated thoughts somewhere along the line. Occulture abounds.

There is presently also a strong resurgence or romanticism when it comes to cottage industries, as in the emergence of a new cassette culture, vital vinyl editions, and fanzine publishing, including anachronistic use of Risographs and vintage Xerox machines. Again, we can't say that TOPY deserves all the praise for this movement, because that would simply be too grandiose a statement. But the occurrence in itself certainly points nostalgically to a time when there was a massive and substantial pre-Internet expression of intimate philosophies, forgotten gems, as well as magical and/or marginal art rather than some kind of soulless mass-production manifestations.

4

Over the Moon and Back Again

Originally published in the Danish magazine Plethora *(No. 5, 2016).*

If your head explodes with dark forebodings too
I'll see you on the dark side of the moon.

PINK FLOYD, "BRAIN DAMAGE"

IT ISN'T EASY BEING HUMAN. Although we live longer and are helped along by technology and pharmaceuticals, we have no guarantee for either happiness or understanding of ourselves during a lifetime of pressure and stress. Where to look for guidance and insight? Well, there are basically two ways to go: in and out. Being introspective can certainly bring insights, but most often only touching upon the individual sphere. If we instead look outside and far away, we can see. . . . Yes what, exactly?

When the sun sets, we are wrapped in darkness and despair. Space is empty, black, enormous, containing myriad tiny, tiny starlights, and allegedly filled with devouring black holes, threatening asteroids, and aliens. Although science can explain things we can't directly perceive with our senses, we are still sensory driven more than anything else.

Always have been, always will be. When the sun rises, the senses are alerted. We can see what's tangible, beneficial, detrimental, and we can make sober evaluations based on rational processes. Most of us structure our active lives based on the visibility of the sun and then retract when it's no longer visible. One could say this is natural, in the sense of *natural* for optimal utilitarian use of the waking state.

But of course there is light also at night. We usually don't see it because of all our own artificial lights. But the fact that it's actually there provides primordial comfort. The moon, reflecting the sun that is currently busy elsewhere, has been the true guiding light for humans all along history. At times, during full eclipses, we may claim to be fascinated by a phenomenon in the sky. But in actual fact we're instinctually terrified.

The sun affects us by heat and light in very direct, tangible ways. We take the sun for granted and adapt our lives and cultures around it. The moon, however, affects us by reflected light and magnetic force— quite a different story. The sun may permit life but the moon regulates it and thereby controls human destiny to a greater and more tangible extent.

The reflected light of the moon isn't brutally revealing but faint, suggestive, ocularly conducive to tricks and impressions of association and fantasy. This reflected light is also conducive to beauty in that it lessens contrast and thereby inherent dualisms. This has been well used in our own recent culture through the development of photography and cinema, in which lighting techniques (an entire science!) very seldom focus on harsh, direct light but rather on subtle nuances of reflected light.

Because the sun is simply too bright to watch, we have become accustomed to watching the moon instead. We cherish what's visible and fear what's invisible. And as we know, anything regular is a comfort to the human mind. In the case of the moon, it's literally so. It's not just a fairly familiar orb in the sky. We literally see the same side of the full moon most every time we watch it. The full moon always displays the same side to us as it revolves around its own axis parallel to its revolving around the earth, and that takes just about the same amount of time. No wonder then we're as fascinated by the dark side of the moon as we are by the dark side of ourselves.

As the human gaze has gradually drifted from the macrocosmic to the microcosmic over the millennia, we have also downsized our capacity for understanding bigger contexts. For the sake of convenient storytelling, symbols in mythology used to consist of the most powerful and potent forces dressed in human or godly shape. Today, sadly, we're striving for a brutal demythologizing process through technologies that allow neither longevity nor potent symbolism. Where is the mythological moon today?

All cultures have revered the moon, most of them as a feminine force in joint ventures with the masculine sun. Of course there are exceptions to the rule: the German language has the moon as masculine and the sun as feminine, and in many Eskimo stories the moon is a strong masculine force and the sun a warm, life-giving feminine force (not surprising perhaps, if one takes the Greenlandish climate into account!).

A key to mythological strength is the use of symbols within the stories told. No wonder that the sun and the moon have been such strong presences in human stories that most often retell sexual tales and death-and-rebirth mysteries. Any pantheon worthy of its name contains gods and goddesses attributed to the stronger forces out there in space. Moon goddesses abound. One of the first occurrences of moon divinities is actually a male one: the Babylonian god Sin. But from there and on, it's been mostly goddesses.

Speculation about why this is can essentially only remain speculation. The most predominant argument is physiological-biological. The cyclic nature of the moon's presence and visibility has always been easy for humans to interpret (rather than that of, say, Mars or Jupiter). The menstrual cycle of women normally sticks to a regularity of four weeks, and this fact must have been easily observable and transmittable very early on: hence an association that extended into culture. The ebb and tide of the sea also became attributed (correctly) to lunar forces, and could easily have been extended association-wise to the ebb and flow of menstruation and its ties to (in)valuable new life.

The Mediterranean cultures worshiped the moon reverently through its goddesses. The Egyptian Isis, the Greek Selene, the Roman Diana, and so on, cross-fertilized at night over time in mythic minds, and other pagan pantheons all over the world had already done that, and were/are still doing it. Aega, Aine, Anahita, Andromeda, Anunit, Arianrhod, Artemis, Arawa, Athenesic, Auchimalgen, Benids, Britomartis, Candi, Cerridwen, Chang-O, Coyolxauhqui, Dae-Soon, Gnatoo, Gwaten, Epona, Hanwi, Hecate, Hina Hine, Hina-Ika, Huitaco, Ishtar, Ix Chel, Izanami, Jezanna, Juna, Jyotsna, Komorkis, Kuan Yin, Lasya, Lucina, Luna, Mama Quilla, Mawu, Metzli, Rhiannon, Sadarnuna, Sarpandit, Sefkhet, Sina, Teczistecatl, Trivia, Xochhiquetzal, Yemanja, Yolkai Estsan, Zirna . . . The list may not be endless but it's extensive enough to show how essential the moon goddess has always been in all insightful cultures. One indicative monotheistic demoting we find in the word *trivial,* stemming from the Roman goddess Trivia, and today indicating something unimportant and irrelevant. Another is the fact that the iconography of the powerful crescent moon associated with Luna and Diana later on became a symbol of chastity in the Virgin Mary.

The sexualization of planets via gods and goddesses is a language and process of necessity. If there is no myth circling around outer phenomena that are beyond our control, then despair quickly sets in. If there is no elevation or augmentation of banal, human toil into divine shape, then ditto. The merging of the masculine and feminine principles stemming from the immensely powerful cosmic forces and filtered through divine idealizations via myth is a safeguard for the human psyche—one that's presently and hopefully only temporarily lost.

A higher awareness of the human mind itself, and of the necessity of an advanced open-minded culture, flourished during the (mainly Italian) Renaissance. Art and literature bloomed, and quite often with inspired strings attached to antiquity's pantheonic health. Revitalized Neoplatonism catapulted both sciences and arts into a zone of esoteric open-mindedness and optimism. Add some book-printing progress to that, and the mythic reinforcement by cosmic iconographies added to the allure of what the Catholic Church had tried in vain to ban: a benevolent bouquet of human qualities rather than a monotheistic terror clutch. The richly detailed symbols of medieval alchemical imagery reintroduced the cosmic elements into human culture, and with that an appreciation of gods and goddesses rather than just one stern patriarchal force.

Paintings commissioned or sanctioned by open-minded princely courts could reintegrate an overt cosmic approach. The setting was usually simple: the sun and the moon affect human life, and we understand the connections via magic, astrology, and tolerance rather than via the Christian iconography of death and torture. In many ways, the Renaissance was a cultural rebirth made possible by the cosmic forces themselves, albeit in symbolic form.

One of the most beautiful images depicting this cosmic revitalization is Cristoforo de Predis's fifteenth-century masterpiece *De Sphaera* (*Of the Spheres*). The section dealing with the moon depicts a beautiful naked woman within a concentric orb containing several other circular shapes. The biggest one, a foundation, contains a crab, symbolizing Cancer (the astrological sphere ruled over by the moon). Covering the woman's sex is a lunar figure, serene and most often associated with the Greek goddess Selene. In her left hand is a torch symbolizing the dark-moon goddess Hecate, and in her right Diana's hunting horn. Around her orb we see sky and sea, filled with waves and ships dependent on her visibility and grace for navigation and keeping time.

Thanks to the regularity of the moon's visibility, we have adapted our structuring of time itself around her. Although we now have a larger (solar) 365-day calendar, we still live and work in lunar weeks, with four weeks making a full lunar month, and the first day of every week being the Moon's Day (Monday, Måndag, Montag, Lundi, etc.).

But no matter what, nighttime is the right time. The beauty of nighttime illuminated by the moon in any of her phases accentuates the feminine connection. The dispersion of daytime's contrast and hard shadows allows for a more poetic frame of mind, in which courtship, wooing, secret meetings, erotic pleasures, and so forth, are more likely to take place. All through human history, the moon has been associated with poetry as well as both sexual and romantic love: a swarming and looser mind frame made possible by the cool, suggestive softness of the night sky.

The negative aspect of the (mainly) full moon has been mythically captured in different cultures in the phenomenon of lycanthropy, that is, werewolves running wild. In many ways, this is a balance, albeit uncontrolled, to the feminine serenity. Lycanthropy can in many ways be seen as a form of male hysteria, set free by maximum exposure to the bright feminine light in the darkness, in which the primordial beast in the male goes on a rapacious rampage.

Other kinds of moon madness also occur in slightly milder forms, and have been validated throughout history in myths and accounts—but also in legislation. The Lunacy Act in England, formulated in 1845, "defined a lunatic as a demented person enjoying lucid intervals during the first two phases of the moon, and 'afflicted with a period of fatuity in the period following the full moon.'"[1] Today, we instead apply a sociopsychological model/matrix to criminal behavior in line with our utilitarian, causal, anthropocentric worldview. But does this imply that the moon no longer affects criminals (or others)? Of course not.

The race to actually, physically, get to the moon is an intriguing piece of history, preceded by thousands of fictional (and thereby mythical) accounts. As science fiction culture in pulp magazines, books, and their cinematic counterparts boomed during the first half of the twentieth century, the generations growing up with it all were saturated by their own dreams turned incentives. Everything begins in fantasy, myth, and fiction, and space travel is certainly no exception from the rule. However, the actual facts make the mind boggle, jog, and spin like a rocket out of control.

Adolf Hitler's attempts to destroy resistance from the British Isles during the final stages of the Second World War saw the development of the V2 rocket (later on mythologized in Thomas Pynchon's techno-sexual absurdist drama *Gravity's Rainbow*). The main engineer behind this powerful rocket-missile was Wernher von Braun. As soon as the war was over, the formerly pro-Nazi scientists of von Braun's team weren't put on trial but rather safely escorted to the United States and given top positions to develop their craft further.

In 1954, Walt Disney produced three films for his television series *Disneyland,* all focusing on space travel: *Man in Space, Man and the Moon,* and *Mars and Beyond.* The first show was aired in 1955 and was viewed by 100 million people—half of the American population at the time. The consultants and technical producers of the show were Wernher von Braun, Heinz Haber, Ernst Stuhlinger, and Willy Ley (a rocket aficionado who had actually fled from Nazi Germany in 1935. Parallel to developing rocket theories and experiments in the United States during the 1940s, he was also an avid science fiction/space travel writer). One of the 100 million people who watched this episode was Dwight D. Eisenhower, at that time president of the United States. He borrowed a copy of the film and showed it at the Pentagon. That in itself became the launch (pardon the pun) of the American space program, in that it facilitated the development of the first ever American satellite—and then some! Government officials were apparently as fascinated by the mix of rocket science and science fiction as were many other Americans. And Russians too, of course. This was in the midst of the Cold War, and the potential scenario of being able to blast an accursed enemy from space was enthusiastically funded by governments, now that Walt Disney had set the stage together with ex-Nazi scientists.

Moon and space myths now quickly became more and more advanced, reflecting the actual goings-on in labs and silos of secrecy. No doubt these were fueled further in the 1960s by mass consumption of LSD in younger generations, with the epitomical trip (again, pardon the pun) being Stanley Kubrick's 1968 sci-fi masterpiece *2001*. This film not only takes us into outer space but also into inner space, and actualizes the dilemma that we today unfortunately exist in: what happens when computers start talking back and controlling us rather than the initial vice versa? The visual brilliance of this film led Kubrick, according to himself, into a quagmire of vanity mixed with dread.

In July of 1969, the entire world (or at least the parts with access to television) sat entranced at images of the first moon landing. The Russian vessel *Luna 9* had transmitted photographs from the lunar surface already in 1966, and the United States followed suit with *Lunar Orbiter 1.* This was mainly to check out the surface: Where would be a good place to actually land? In December 1968, the American *Apollo 8,* a manned spacecraft, reached the moon's orbit and then returned home. The crew read from the book of Genesis on their Christmas Eve television special—at the time the most watched television program ever.[2] This very likely in anticipation of what was to come. On July 20, 1969, new television records were set. A fifth of the world's population watched Neil Armstrong and Buzz Aldrin walk on the moon—*allegedly* walk on the moon, if we listen to Stanley Kubrick.

Lunar ecstasy for certain, but the modern myths didn't end with Armstrong's "giant leap for mankind." When Stanley Kubrick died in 1999, he died with a secret he had leaked just a little. According to his own myth, he had been hired by NASA after the success of *2001* to fake the images being broadcast from the lunar landing. His visual acumen and dramaturgic brilliance apparently created a very convincing moon landing and moon walk. Whether this deception is actually true or not is as unlikely to surface as the truth about 9/11. But in Kubrick's paranoid mind, there was a discrepancy between leaking and fearing assassination and keeping silent in deceit. "I perpetrated a huge fraud," Kubrick revealed in a 1999 interview.[3] And he then insisted the interviewer not show this material until at least fifteen years after Kubrick's death.

Again, the moon had proven an instrumental part of human mythology and the (possible) illusion of progress. Again, the moon had been a reflective surface spurring on poetic visions of power, regardless if truthful or not. Caspar David Friedrich and other German romantic "Sturm und Drangers" used canvas and paint to catch the suggestive power of the moon, setting it into contexts in which the human being was always very small; smaller than awe-inspiring life and the cosmos itself. With technology, of rockets and television alike, the perspective has changed, making human ingenuity (read: hubris) larger than life— possibly even larger than actual truth.

The space race has become a phallic striving for triumph—not so much a quest for human ideals as a conquest of assets and resources. In many ways, the reflective surface of the moon has illuminated a technological lycanthropy in which space is the place and the television medium is still the message in itself. Massive exploitation will take place but the main thing for the common folks will be the various reality shows broadcast more or less live from outer space, with the moon as the first network and space-shuttle service station.

The moon doesn't only teach us about our relationship to ourselves in space but also in time. The very same reflective surface we look at today shone its clear light on Novalis, Friedrich, Goethe, all the worshipers of moon goddesses, witches in dim groves, lovers in medieval sagas, covert conspirators who changed the world, on Dion Fortune (*Moon Magic*), Aleister Crowley (*Moonchild*), Kenneth Anger (*Rabbit's Moon*), and on the songwriters of "Moon River," "Blue Moon", "Harvest Moon," "Fly Me to the Moon," "Bad Moon Rising," and so on.

The few cosmic constants we have certainly put things in healthy perspective—if only we allow them to. If we don't, and just take them for granted while drifting into artificialities and abstractions, their magic will wane and we will be ostracized from the ebb and flow of natural processes and cycles. That's essentially the curse of the human being: not seeing her right place in the totality, and instead looking for causal shortcuts in petty power struggles. The wisdom of the moon is obvious: life is cyclical and regular. The early humans realized this as they learned how to survive by adapting to the cycles of the year or, in the case of women, to the cycles of the lunar month. The basic facts of life still revolve around lunar forces, whether basic (a human embryo is developed during nine lunar months) or cultural/religious:

> In 325 CE the Council of Nicaea established that Easter would be held on the first Sunday after the first full moon occurring on or after the vernal equinox. From that point forward, the Easter date depended on the ecclesiastical approximation of March 21 for the vernal equinox. Easter is delayed by one week if the full moon is on Sunday, which decreases the chances of it falling on the same day as the Jewish Passover. The council's ruling is contrary to the Quartodecimans, a group of Christians who celebrated Easter on the day of the full moon, 14 days into the month.[4]

These Judeo-Christian rites and celebrations are all remains of earlier pagan customs, which just goes to show that the awareness of the moon's presence and potency was fully integrated in pre-Christian times. Today, it's a different story, with the main reflective light coming from computer and television screens. Contemplating a full moon on a clear night brings out/up things from the hidden strata of the soul. An electronic screen can never compete, because it's relying on the content someone else places on that screen. The longer the distance from the moon (in both time and space) that new generations experience, the less likely it is that the human contemplative ability will remain as such. If a capacity isn't used and exercised, it will dwindle and die.

That said, the moon might then actually be a seemingly passive yet covertly very active counterforce to this contemporary negation of life. Women in general, artists, sensitives, and poets throughout history have been highly aware of the moon and its relevance, and have adapted to it in humility and inspiration. Again, the lycanthropic filter needs to be applied. "Moon madness" of varying degrees and cultural shapes signifies the inability to handle certain aspects of the human psyche: sensitivity, inspiration, nonutilitarian creativity, and so on. The response becomes compensating and "solar-phallic" (as Crowley would term it): aggressive, rapacious, and feral. For the insensitive, the moon becomes something pallid, useless, and terrifying in its mysteriousness, something you sleep away from in awaiting the return of the sun, which makes everything bright and simple again. It is interesting to note how the myth of the werewolf is also soaked in blood. This ferocity and bloodlust, essentially male in essence, in combination with a female shedding of blood presided over by lunar forces and relating to fertility, would make Sigmund Freud and later psychoanalysts nod their heads. Perhaps not in approval of the phenomenon itself but certainly as a validation of the theory that sex and aggression are two sides of the same coin.

Where much has been written about human development and dietary habits in times when vegetarians and carnivores coexisted, and somehow applying a simplified matriarchy-versus-patriarchy filter, I believe that much of the werewolf mythology in relation to the moon simply stems from early human sexual trauma. Even somewhat peaceful vegetarian-agrarian tribes could defend themselves better in the daytime against ferocious human enemies. But at night, with the serene moon acting as an existential twilight, it was easier to attack, loot, and rape. The survival instinct is not a static constant. It keeps on developing and is transmitted onward, partly in DNA and partly through mythology, to help future generations survive. The strong association between nighttime, the moon, blood, and sexual assault is not a consciously formulated fear or pleasure to take lightly. It's ingrained deeply within us.

> The idea that it is "sinful" to shed the blood that is "life"—retained in the course of the transition from the vegetarian to the carnivore—and the belief that expiatory rites are required to avert the dangers connected with a practice that it was never really intended to abandon, since its results had proved so advantageous to the lupine pack, caused a consciousness of "sin" and a need for apotropaic ceremonies to attach itself even to the effusion of blood resulting from sexual intercourse with virgins. These the aggressive pack would, whenever occasion offered, kidnap and carry away from among the females of the weaker fruit-gathering tribes so as by this new practice of "exogamy" to avoid the otherwise inevitable, risky fight with the leader of the wolf-pack claiming for himself the females of the lupine clan.[5]

Georgs Méliès's short but incredibly beautiful film *A Trip to the Moon* (1902) not only blew minds at the time but is still in many ways emblematic of the human perspective: we can conquer the "challenge" by technology and enthusiasm, but we look at the process as a causal adventure more than as an opportunity to truly learn about ourselves. Méliès adapted his story from H. G. Wells's *The First Men in the Moon* (1901) and Jules Verne's *From the Earth to the Moon* (1865), and turned it into a simple story of naive optimism. In the film, a group of scientists debate and discuss going to the moon. They build a rocket that successfully lifts off, travels in space and then hits the man in the moon right in the eye, which serves as an entry point into the moon proper. The crew suddenly find themselves in a cave filled with mushrooms (not unlike psilocybin 'shrooms), and are taken by force to the moon court by guards more or less dressed up as devilish skeletons. When these guards are attacked, they go up in a cloud of smoke, as theatrical illusions of sorts. It all seems threatening enough, and the crew escapes the same way they came: in their rocket, through space and back to earth.

As science fiction progressed parallel to the technical developments that suddenly and actually could take us to the moon, the perspective became more dystopian and bleak rather than the opposite (Kubrick's *2001* is a philosophical masterpiece also in this respect). The mythological aspects carry optimism; the real, a considerably darker hue. If we look at science fiction as the true seed and facilitator of actual space travel, this latter-day dystopian perspective should be regarded as a prophetic warning of sorts. If myth and fiction always precede real developments, where are all the optimistic sunshine stories of successful life in space nowadays? Méliès may have displayed a prophecy in more ways than one, albeit in a humorous way. Yes, we can go to the moon (and back) but perhaps it's after all best instead to look at the moon as a symbol of desire and reflective surface rather than think we can "master" it and then have to face the skeletal cave dwellers of the unknown. Art not only reflects its zeitgeist but also amplifies what is reflected, for better or worse.

The artistic reflection and brilliance of the Renaissance painters and medieval alchemical engravers, integrating cosmic wisdom for the sake of illumination via symbols, is a peak in human culture that we'll very likely never experience again. It is indeed very strange that although we have made such enormous progress in the fields of science and technology, it seems as most of it is designed to facilitate a non-reflective, "easier" lifestyle and the vain hopes of either a longer life or life in space. The outer perspective thus takes precedence. But history shows, as does mythology in general, that the inner route may be the wiser one. The mere aspect of light seen through the symbolic should make this clear. The stronger the light (as in *solar*), the stronger the shadow. This carries with it an inherent dualism that is certainly well-known to the human psyche but, unfortunately, seemingly difficult to cope with. A faint lunar light decreases the contrast and thereby opens up the mind to inner insights and deeper feelings than simply "fight or flight."

A reality show is currently being prepared for the journey to Mars. Without a doubt, the ratings will soar when the vessel eventually takes off into space. Ridley Scott's *The Martian* (starring Matt Damon) shows the real dilemma in an über-heroic way: What happens when things go wrong? What breaks down first—technology or the human psyche? *The Martian* is a demagogic example for simpletons of wishful thinking, or the same kind of naive optimism that Méliès displayed in regard to his moon. The mythological view has been abandoned for human hubris yet again, and nothing good will come of that. When things go wrong on that upcoming Martian vessel—and believe me, they will—the ratings of that reality show will undoubtedly soar even more. Incidentally, it was Ridley Scott's amazingly dystopian *Alien* (1979) that was marketed with the slogan "In space no one can hear you scream"—a prophecy, no doubt, televised or not.

As always, we believe what we see, but we need light to see it. Preferably it should be reflected from an untainted lunar surface on a clear and starry night. That should be quite enough.

5

Pokémon Go Away

Originally published in the Norwegian magazine
Kunstforum (No. 3, 2016).

IN OUR POST-POSTMODERN CULTURE, the definitions of what can be deemed "art" have become more and more flexible. Where gradually wider creative phenomena like fashion, design, and architecture have approached and entered the arena of accepted art, art's essence (instigating magical change through aestheticized personal expression, thereby enhancing the experience of life) has become more and more pushed away by superficialities and mass-market adaptation—no doubt reflecting the overall contemporary culture as a whole.

This constitutes a problem, and not only on the level of terminology. The problem consists of a demoting of an essential sphere or phenomenon into a commodified area that mainly uses the rational mind to evaluate even aesthetic or emotional spheres. To use an example closer to the core question: art is art, but the art world is not art. The rational handling of and trading with something stemming from the soul doesn't make the actual handling or trading soulful. But unfortunately this is what has happened, and it's continuing to de-enchant and demythologize the world as we know it.

Art has been the main carrier of human mythologies, which is

51

one reason why it can be called essential. Without substantial and relevant stories created for inspiration, teaching, reflection, and resonance humans would still just be base, instinct-driven animals. This mythologizing quality is essentially what sets us apart from other animals (not forgetting the complex and in this case almost paradoxical phenomenon of suicide). The meeting of human minds and stories is what defines the very concept of being human.

There is also the tricky but ingenious aspect of art as a more general human endeavor, which is something that has helped our contemporary confusion along. Creative skills have always been used for working *in the now* through organized crafts, which means creating memes that *define the now.* Fashion, design, architecture, and writing in general have been integrated as parts of active and creative history writing, and definitely with the *potential* to tell mythological stories in a mosaic kind of way. But it's only recently that these crafts have attempted to invade a more substantial mythological arena. Why is this?

I would say that technology is to blame, followed closely by greed. A new definition or packaging of an old phenomenon helps sell it again. The onslaught of technology has drained human existence of genuine mythological force. The massive commercial potential in the smaller, faster, cheaper constructs/platforms, filled with smaller, faster, cheaper content, inevitably affects us all in negative ways. It's hard to see the big picture on a small screen. I'm not in any way implying a conspiracy to dumb down human intelligence, but unfortunately this is the inevitable result of a process that reflects a species that has basically negated its libido and reshaped it into a frantic death drive.

In his excellent book *Creative Mythology–The Masks of God,* Joseph Campbell once listed four key functions of mythology:

1. The reconciliation of consciousness with the preconditions of its own existence. Handling the often sorrowful realization

that human existence is temporal. The creation of an ideal, the "other," the holy/religious

2. The formulating and rendering of a cosmological image of the universe in keeping with the science of the time and of such a kind that, within its range, all things should be recognized as parts of a single great holy picture

3. The validation and maintaining of some specific social order, authorizing its moral code as a construct beyond criticism or human emendation

4. The psychological angle: shaping individuals to the aims and ideals of their various social groups

If we look at the contemporary scene with the help of this specific model, and integrate both what I would call "real" art and the more ephemeral creative crafts listed above, it's not a pretty picture. The escapistic longing of people for definitive, holy, authoritarian, religious ideas has created a violent global instability, and the mythological expressions are simplified in extreme dualisms of good versus bad. The previously helpful cosmological image no longer looks at the inspiring as well as awe-inspiring grand-scale totality but at the ever-smaller particles—an escapist analysis of the intangibly minute only possible via technology. Social order is maintained by ever-stricter control, either blatantly dictatorial or via diametrical manipulations (freedom of expression more monitored than ever, freedom of movement scrutinized by surveillance, freedom of thought made ill at ease by the doublespeak of political correctness).

The fourth point is perhaps the most interesting one. Although our Western cultural sphere officially lauds equality and the nobility of mobility, the tools we use actually stratify more than ever before. Some decades ago, one used to say that access to computers was a class issue. Today, the opposite is true—the person who can afford to be out of reach of technology is at the top of the existential pyramid.

Education via fiction, and this predominantly via technology, has created a greater class divide than ever before, as the need for noncritical human slaves/machine operators increases. And as technology itself is on its way to reshaping work life (more "free" time for humans means more possibilities/time to consume and be even more enslaved) we will rapidly approach the pivotal moment that science fiction writers have been obsessed with for centuries: the dreaded power switch when intelligent machines become sentient and thereby ruled by self-preservation rather than human authority.

A recent visit to New York provided much fodder for thought about this for me. This was not only in the usual and quite endearing American way ("Wow, this is the biggest chocolate chip cookie ever!" uttered a child who received the cookie in question from the waiter when her parents were busy paying for lunch; the customer care that goes to any length, even potential diabetes, to ensure a safe return not home but to the restaurant in question) but rather more of a morose kind. On a busy street corner I saw three boys and one adult man. They were all clutching their cell phones, staring into them and then nervously up at "reality." "There!" one boy shouted. "No, there!" shouted another. The adult looked as nervous and giddy as the boys. I realized they were playing Pokémon Go, and after an initial fascination, the scene depressed me. Despite the frenzy, the passivity was so total; their minds so completely immersed in a digital fantasy world alluringly mixed with so-called real-world landscapes. The invasion of the private sphere has now apparently gone public. It's a dissolution of human dignity and a fictional entrapment that I fear will not be temporary.

When visiting the Museum of Modern Art, I was pleasantly overwhelmed by the exhibitions: a Bruce Conner retrospective, items from Tony Oursler's truly magical collections, Nan Goldin's *The Ballad of Sexual Dependency* series, and a display of Tristan Tzara and Francis Picabia's *DadaGlobe* material. It was such a great display of art at its very best: evocative, intelligent, humorous, beautiful, transcending time, thought-provoking, and more. This visit was unfortunately balanced out perfectly by one to its sister museum, MoMA PS1. Where MoMA is "modern," PS1 is "contemporary." Although I entered with an open mind, the entire experience was intimidating and even more depressing than the Pokémon Go gang. It was floor upon floor of soulless displays of mental constructs. A lot of the works shown at the time of my visit supposedly celebrated the origins of the PS1 "concept," with a focus on 1970s performance art. In this, the postmodern lingo runs amok in abstractions and explanations that shouldn't really be needed if the art itself packed a mythological punch. But this is the arena not of visionary artists but of curators and collectors, defining spheres that really need no middlemen (or women) at all. It's a sterile display celebrating superficiality and smartness rather than aestheticism and intelligence. Great art should need no externalized context.

The displayed photos of Chinese artist Deng Tai nocturnally draped in a red flag are quite beautiful in themselves. But when they become contextualized and, even worse, politicized, the mythology potential dwindles: "Deng is at once visible and illegible, bare and costumed, a fugitive body enacting a private theater in which he is both performer and audience." Papo Colo: "The MoMA PS1 presentation centers around Colo's *Superman 51* (1977), in which he drags a collection of fifty-one white pieces of wood behind him, tethered to his body with ropes, as he runs shirtless down an empty stretch of Manhattan's West Side Highway until collapsing from exhaustion."

Who are these descriptions for? Is it impossible for the works of art to be self-explanatory or communicate via a mythological language that bars that of the curators? Images and symbols usually make more sense than clarifications and elaborations. I kept thinking of the psychology of reality shows on TV, where we first see what goes on, and then have it explained to us by one or often several of the participants. It's a repetition of the already given that makes it hard (if not impossible) to make up your own mind. And perhaps that's exactly the point of these dehumanized and de-enchanted pseudomythologies?

Almost as if to humor my prejudices in regard to the scene's condescending predictability, the main exhibition, Vito Acconci's 1976 *Where Are We Now (And Who Are We Anyway?)*, is described with accentuations like "Since the mid-'80s through the present, Acconci has mixed with a design and architecture studio." Why am I not surprised that this is stressed? Acconci's hard work as a performance artist becomes utterly trivialized as the curators sprinkle evanescent lifestyle terms. That's what happens when self-serving academics steal the show, and that's exactly how essentially great art loses its mythological punch-packing.

6

What Remains for the Future?

An Initial Attempt at a Comparison between Aleister Crowley and Rudolf Steiner

Originally a lecture delivered at the Lashtal Conference in Gdansk, Poland, 2013.

LOOKING BACK AT the twentieth century, we can see that it was probably one of the most intense centuries ever. Regardless which kinds of glasses we put on to watch our own contemporary history closer, it's easy to see that the twentieth century was phenomenal and revolutionary in many ways.

Aleister Crowley claimed that 1904 was an especially pivotal year, as that was the year he had authored or "received" his key text, *The Book of the Law.* By declaring the Law of Thelema and the Aeon of Horus (the child) Crowley positioned himself as prophet and interpreter through devoting his life and efforts to informing and, hopefully, enlightening others. He was pretty good at it, too. His efforts have actually brought us together here today, which is indeed a magical thing.

However, Crowley was far from alone in the participation of this aeonic shift. Several others presented similar ideas: individualism, cosmic altruism, breaking away from too-rigid cultural and religious structures, an integration of alternative spiritual methods that had up until the shift been looked upon as suspect and heretical, and so on. On the whole, the zeitgeist included a holistic spirituality that integrated thoughts, ideas, and methods from other cultures, predominantly Asian. Theosophy was one main movement, that stemming from Gurdjieff and his disciples was another.

Crowley's own Herculean labor of giving birth to this new aeon has recently been well documented in several biographies, and I think most of us know his story fairly well: An initial curiosity about all things magical and esoteric, a firsthand experience of philosophical systems and religious approaches through his travels, a will to inform and enlighten through his *Equinox* volumes, in which he also divulged the secrets of the previous kings of the hill, the Hermetic Order of the Golden Dawn, and then working with the Thelemic orders the A∴A∴ and the OTO, as well as writing ambitiously (to say the least).

Although plagued by a great number of personal issues and problems, the impression we get of Crowley is still one of great devotion and self-discipline. Whether Thelema will become a major religion or philosophy in the future we have yet to see. But if we stick with the human being Crowley for now, we can see that he is currently about as established as he can be. He is out there, present in contemporary consciousness, but perhaps more for his fascinating life story than for Thelema as a philosophy or religious system.

Another important interpreter and innovator of the same New Age shift was Austrian Rudolf Steiner (1861–1925). His Anthroposophy has many similarities with Thelema. I'm going to try to point out some similarities, and also some differences, in order to shine the light on how it is that these two movements have both been quite successful but in very different ways and to varying degrees.

Steiner for a long time contained his own individual enlightenment, which was a result of thinking, feeling, and willing but also of contacts with a spiritual master/teacher earlier on. When the time came for him to eventually blossom, during his successful career within Theosophy, he bloomed with a great appetite for sharing what he had experienced on the inner planes. He too became good at that. Theosophy was soon no longer enough for him, and he created his own system and school, Anthroposophy, just as Crowley had done after the Golden Dawn experiences and the reception of *The Book of the Law*. Initially an academic specializing in Goethe studies, Steiner gradually developed into a very creative polymath who also had the ability to enthuse people to help him out.

Crowley published his ten massive *Equinox* volumes between 1909 and 1913, under the banner of Scientific Illuminism and the motto "The method of science, the aim of religion." Steiner called his method Spiritual Science, and also wrote and lectured intensely to inform the interested. In this sense, both men were very much alike. Crowley was certainly more of a rebel, but they shared an ego-transcending will to improve mankind through the integration of nonrational phenomena within a contemporary and very rational mind frame, thereby bringing occult and spiritual ideas from both the outer and inner worlds into contact with modern society and its empirical standards and critical demands.

Essentially, their wisdoms are one and the same:

- A human being has the potential to become enlightened and fully individual. One method of achieving this is to trust one's own intuition and be guided in inner spheres by strata of consciousness previously unacknowledged.
- A human being has the potential to set standards for others and inspire them to explore themselves through this process of self-trust. Altruism happens by proxy.
- A holistic integration of various human expressions (science, art, culture, religion, etc.) into this overall philosophy will also benefit and further mankind by setting new stages and standards.

- A pragmatic synthesis will result from the holistic integration of teachings from different cultural spheres. Examples include the integration of yoga and meditation within a basically Western mind frame (Christianity in Steiner's case, Qabalistic mysticism in Crowley's).

Basically, we're seeing a teaching that empowers the individual to see the bigger picture, something that will help others too, either by concrete measures or by inspiration. Trusting one's inner experiences and non-rational, esoteric processes is of vital importance in both cases. These must, however, be tested by empirical research and validated by usefulness in spheres larger than the merely individual. Phenomena that had previously been regarded as hocus-pocus or even superstitiously as the Devil's work were now becoming substantial parts of entire systems of philosophy for normal people from all walks of life. Communicating with angels, elemental entities, astral intelligences, and so on, were suddenly presented as not only matters of fact but also as recommended practices for better self-knowledge and development for modern people.

Crowley used *The Book of the Law* and Thelema as springboards for applications and implementations on different fields of human behavior and existence but seldom got further than theoretical blueprints. Steiner, on the other hand, networked intensely with people who had both assets and ideas of their own. For instance, the collaboration with the altruistic cigarette manufacturer Emil Molt initiated the first Waldorf school at Molt's Waldorf-Astoria factory in Stuttgart in 1919. Today, there are more than one thousand Waldorf schools worldwide. The construction of the first Goetheanum building in Dornach (Steiner's spiritual teaching center) was begun in 1913 but the building unfortunately burnt down in 1922. The building of the new Goetheanum, this time constructed of concrete, was finished in 1928. Work on biodynamic farming and gardening was also initiated early on, as were clinical, empirical experiments in Anthroposophic medicine.

Crowley's legacy is basically owed to a handful of individuals who were close to him at some point quite late in his life. I'm thinking specifically of Karl Germer, Grady McMurtry, Gerald Yorke, John Symonds, and Kenneth Grant. If it weren't for the diligent archival obsession of Gerald Yorke, for instance, and his donation to the Warburg Institute at the University of London, invaluable Crowley source material would be lost forever or scattered into the digital abyss of eBay. If it weren't for these other men's exploitation of their own Crowley association, there would be no substantial Crowley presence today. The value of these few contacts, which were essentially uncontrollable for Crowley himself, has of course been enormous. The same is true for the value of Crowley's own publishing efforts.

Gerald Yorke not only donated his vast collection of information and Crowleyana to the Warburg but also earlier on sent duplicates to Germer in the United States and Norman Robb in Australia. Despite this enormous foresight and benevolence, things and papers disappeared along the way, as they tend to do. It seems that the most important thing to leave behind are actually good old-fashioned books.

Incidentally, the first book ever that stirred Yorke's interest in things esoteric was one of Steiner's.[1]

Steiner's legacy, on the other hand, was carefully strategized by himself while still alive. The massive amount of lectures (4,941 lectures are documented, but I don't know if that's even possible; he started out fairly late, around the turn of the century within the Theosophical environment, and then had approximately twenty-five very active years, which would mean some 200 lectures per year) opened doors to new environments and a constant flow of new people in different countries. If even a fraction of these turned out benevolent, it was indeed a successful endeavor. The publishing of his ideas was more or less immediate through presses that were supportive of the movement. The integration into society in the Germanic sphere was of course important and a very logical extension of several decades of German open-mindedness in various forms of *Lebensreform* movements. The Third Reich temporarily put everything in hiatus of course, but not so much in neutral Switzerland, where the Goetheanum maintained its status as the international center of Anthroposophy (which it still is).

Steiner integrated a middle path that could but didn't necessarily "involve a passionate 'union of opposites'" (quoting Crowley in his description of the "magick of Horus"). However, Steiner was indeed aware of the transformative magic of diametrics. His own schematic symbol for the ideal human being was a statue he himself carved out of wood, and which today is displayed at the Goetheanum: *The Representative of Man: Christ between Lucifer and Ahriman.* This gnostic Christ principle balances the ungrounded, spiritual loftiness of Lucifer with its ensuing pride and the gross, Malkuthian materialism of Ahriman. An enlightened being who can balance these very human energies or temptations will have gained insight by the mere effort. If we allow ourselves some philosophically speculative slack within the Thelemic pantheon, the statue could perhaps equally well be called "Ra-Hoor-Khuit between Nuit and Hadit."

Steiner's progressive attitude to Christianity is without a doubt another reason why Anthroposophy has been able to grow and mature without head-on collisions with established powerful and intolerant dogmas. Early on Crowley took on a persona projected on him by his Christian fundamentalist mother: "the Great Beast." That became an image he himself nurtured throughout his life, and his antipathy toward all things Christian became one of many controversial trademarks.

However, from the perspective of religious or philosophical studies, Thelema is a decidedly neo-Gnostic system. The incentive for and manifestation of enlightenment is individual. Steiner intuited and put forth exactly the same idea. But Steiner's specific psychological fundament had no need of distancing itself from the religion that had prevailed up until the twentieth century, and not infrequently through violence and oppression. Steiner analyzed the Christian mysteries and myths thoroughly and regarded in particular the human being Jesus's Golgothan experience, when he was acting as an enlightened Christ, a gnostic master, as the single most influential happening of the past aeon. This should be regarded solely from a magical, transformative perspective though, not a dogmatic Christian one. Steiner and Anthroposophy are more in debt to Neoplatonism, pantheism, the Renaissance thinkers, and Goethe than to any kind of dogmatic Christian church.

Interesting to note in regard to Thelema as a cosmology with a strong solar presence through Ra Hoor Khuit is that the Christ principle in Steiner's mythology is imbued with distinctly solar force filtered through the archangel Michael. The Golgotha experience is, in Steiner's eyes, not so much an individual self-sacrifice to redeem other people's "sins" as it is a conduction of solar energy into the earth.

What remains if we look at their main ways of expressing themselves? Both men were voluminous writers, and basically everything there is has been made available for a hungry market—in Crowley's case recently but very ambitiously, in Steiner's case all along for decades. The availability of published works these days not only has to do with spreading the words per se but also with income for the respective organizations. There is a substantial value in both men's writings, and especially now that copyright issues are more complex and floating than ever. The copyright holders are eager to maintain a presence on the market. That the books are published in high-quality editions and translations secures both revenue and interest.

Let's not forget that both men were also visual artists. Steiner was inspired by Goethe in more ways than one and ambitiously tried to convey his own inner visions in visual form. Steiner's paintings and sculptures certainly display his will both to communicate a higher system of aesthetics according to Goethe's guidelines, and to have them used for instructional purposes. The main auditorium of the Goetheanum is an impressive, almost incredible, display of this *Gesamt* (total) vision, in which architecture, stained-glass images, mural paintings, light, and acoustics work together to tell a story, teach, and inspire. There are several books focusing on Steiner's visual art available today.

For Steiner, the use of art was ultimately pedagogic and magically strategic: "Beauty is not the divine in a cloak of physical reality; no, it is physical reality in a cloak that is divine. The artist does not bring the divine on to the earth by letting it flow into the world; he raises the world into the sphere of the divine. Beauty is semblance because it conjures before our senses a reality which, as such, appears as an ideal world."[2]

Crowley's paintings, drawings, and the Abbey of Thelema murals at Cefalu were also creative externalizations, although considerably rougher in execution, and there seems to have been no other plan in painting them than simply to paint. Crowley's visual works exist today in private collections, and once in a while, these are exhibited (London 1998, Paris 2008, Australia 2012). A substantial monograph of Crowley as an artist has yet to be published.

Both Steiner and Crowley were extroverts, but for different reasons. Steiner was a distinct Apollonian character by Nietzsche's definition, and Crowley very much a Dionysian one. Crowley wrote well but was inept at handling people not immediately of use to him. Steiner was not the best writer but could deliver inspiring lectures. Crowley was lucky to have a few intelligent people around when he was about to die. And, not forgetting, Crowley's publishing efforts have indeed been talismanically successful. Steiner was more of a structured Germanic mind and basically worked himself to death to secure the immortality of Anthroposophy. His bouquet is considerably larger than Crowley's, and we are all more or less exposed to it when we eat organically produced foods, for instance, or send our kids to Waldorf schools, or use Weleda products. The pioneering research in Steiner's Spiritual Science has definitely made an impact on contemporary culture far more than Crowley's Scientific Illuminism. At least so far.

If one wanted to be a little bit mean-spirited, one could present two parallel images under the umbrella of spiritual centers of the 1920s. One would be a run-down farmhouse in a Sicilian fishing village, its walls painted with obscene poetry and impressionistic demons; the other would be an architecturally advanced and radical building in the Swiss countryside, designed to transmit the spirit of Goethe into the cosmos.

However, it's totally unfair to measure these concepts or systems in terms of quantity and visibility. Crowley's system, after all, is either highly personal and secretive (A∴A∴) or intrafraternal (OTO). The Thelemic environment is more of a private sphere, in which a spiritual, magical attainment is encouraged. Whether that is of any use or interest to anyone else is not relevant unless stated so by the adept in question.

While on the subject of the OTO, I think I should mention too that Steiner met the head of the order at the time, Theodor Reuss, in 1906 in Switzerland—a meeting arranged by leading Theosophist Annie Besant. This was the pre-Thelema OTO of course. These gentlemen found enough common ground to stand on that Steiner became head of an OTO lodge called Mysteria Mystica. Steiner was curious, as he had been about Theosophy, and also sought new environments in which to develop himself as a spiritual teacher. His engagement with OTO phased out quite quickly though. Reuss, Hartmann, and the other early OTO protagonists had a somewhat strange reputation because it was more or less known, even back then, that OTO worked with esoteric tantric sexual rituals in the higher degrees. Perhaps this became too much for Steiner, who was more or less celibate. Anyway, six years later Reuss knocked on Crowley's door, and the rest, as they say, is history. And another reason why we are gathered here today.

At Christmas 1923, Steiner announced to his followers that a new and more ambitious organization, the General Anthroposophical Society, had been set up and that from now on, the publishing of all his lectures was officially sanctioned. Both these developments allowed for a much smoother, and much more public life for the philosophy itself and its many creative offshoots. He also announced a College for Spiritual Science that would teach advanced Anthroposophy at the Goetheanum in Dornach and other places. The name alone makes me think of A∴A∴ as a "College of Scientific Illuminism." There was apparently something in the air that allowed for these teaching structures to manifest on similar lines, regardless of whether they were public or highly secretive.

As the old Anthroposophical Society gave way for this new and better-organized one, Steiner personally issued and signed membership cards for all the old members—twelve thousand of them! And the first big thing to deal with was the rebuilding of the Goetheanum, a large-scale process that actually continued in terms of final decorations well up until the 1990s.

The word *general* is perhaps a magical clue to the success of Anthropsophy after Steiner's death and, of course, especially after the Second World War. Steiner's almost Taoist approach to merge with and augment, improve, develop, and never clash with or use force, allowed for an easy integration into a general mind frame of general society. Sure, some of the ideas of Atlantean civilizations, reincarnation, cosmic farming, eurythmic healing, and so forth, may still be hard to grasp for most people, but no one can deny the common sense of eating biodynamically or at least organically grown food, or the well-documented success of the Waldorf education system, or the Camphill environments for individuals with learning disorders, and so on.

Crowley's attitude was almost diametrical to this: "The key to joy is disobedience." We can never find out if this was willed or if he was making a virtue out of necessity. But I suspect that his drug addiction was the biggest real demon in his life. Not only because of the related financial and physical strains, but because of the will aspect. Although I'm sure he did want to get rid of the addiction, he simply couldn't. We can rationalize and say that just makes him all the more human, sure, but for the Great Beast himself, I believe the persona as the agent provocateur of a new era defined by will was rather unwillingly upheld, and that he would much rather have been someone considerably more welcome in the upper echelons of British society. Crowley's head-on hedonism facilitated a media image that in many ways still lingers on, and it is far from useful to Thelema as a general philosophy that has the potential to transform individual lives, with or without the technology of magic.

It is highly interesting to compare these systems that are so alike in many ways but also so very marked by their creators and their specific psychological traits. And they were both aware of it, for good and bad, and of what lay behind. In both systems, the concepts of karma and reincarnation are present, and both men encouraged their adepts to research previous lives on the inner planes, as they had done themselves. If this research wasn't done properly, one would perhaps have to make similar mistakes over again.

Steiner was unusually clear when he wrote of these principles: "Through memory, the soul preserves yesterday; through action, it prepares tomorrow." And: "As a spiritual being, I must be the repetition of one whose biography can explain mine." And: "I must connect to what I did yesterday if my life is to have order and continuity. Yesterday's actions have become the conditions that regulate what I do today. Through my actions yesterday, I created my destiny for today."[3]

There is in this integration of karma also an accentuation of the holistic. Despite the fact that we are individuals, and we can only really develop on the individual level by gradual refinement, what we do also affects others, and vice versa. These were thoughts that had been around for a long time, even in Europe. John Donne, the seventeenth-century British poet described it well several hundred years before Theosophy: "No man is an island entire of itself; every man is a piece of the continent, a part of the main. . . . Any man's death diminishes me, because I am involved in mankind; and therefore never send to know for whom the bell tolls; it tolls for thee."[4]

Perhaps Donne is a good example in this case, as he too was in between faiths, so to speak. Having been born a Catholic in England, Donne and his family had been exposed to intolerant harassment and even religious murder. When he eventually became a Protestant within the Church of England, he was suddenly lauded and could speak and write freely about almost anything he wished, including the need for tolerance and open-mindedness. It is in a way as if restraint brings an inherent desire for freedom. How this expresses itself has to do mainly with the ego of the person expressing it. Donne was an intelligent opportunist who worked the system to his own benefit. That has benefited us too, as his works and ideas were allowed to remain and survive.

Crowley formulated instructions for the A∴A∴ concerning knowledge of previous incarnations, as that was thought to be essential for magical development. In "Liber 913, Thisharb," he constructed a method for the mind to work backward in order to strengthen the individual memory to the level of transcending the present incarnation: "Memory is essential to the individual consciousness; otherwise the mind were but a blank sheet on which shadows are cast. But we see that not only does the mind retain impressions, but that it is so constituted that its tendency is to retain some more excellently than others."[5]

What remains if we look at other people's memories of these gentlemen? In Crowley's case it depends exclusively on the vantage point of the firsthand writer in question. If Crowley was good to the writer, then the recollection is good. If Crowley was bad or perceived as bad to the writer, then the recollection is bad. A prime example of subjective history writing, and something that was amplified by the fact that he was so infamous as a public figure in the United Kingdom.

It is as if the impressions of the man Crowley are so predominant that more or less objective analyses of his work from his own time are nonexistent. His own descriptions are literally hagiographic (as in his own *Confessions*), and those of, say Fuller or Achad, could easily be seen as hagiographic by proxy. It is mainly during the most recent decades that real Crowley biographies have been written, and these have indeed been very ambitious and well-researched projects.*

In Steiner's case, it is almost as if the person Rudolf Steiner didn't exist. There is, of course, a great deal of hagiographic subjectivity in his case too, but that certainly doesn't stem from himself. He did write an autobiography at the request of his followers, but it is very low-key and basically a chronological recounting of meetings and projects. And, lest we forget, he didn't have the time to finish his own proper biography. It only goes as far as 1907, and that was in many ways when things started to become really interesting in his life. So we are left with other people's accounts of his life, and mostly of the yea-saying variety.

As we can see, there are many similarities between the teachings. Crowley was predominantly interested in the technology of magic and in refining and handling the philosophy of *The Book of the Law*. Steiner was a magnificent visionary who also worked hard at trying the resulting ideas out and making them useful for others. These gentlemen had similar goals but were very different in individual behavior and attitudes. Perhaps we can allow ourselves to regard them as two aspects of the very same phenomenon or entity, like a Horus and Set, a Lucifer and Ahriman, a Christ and a Great Beast, where each facilitates a united dynamic energy in which a human individual can have an uncensored look at him- or herself. This is undoubtedly a fascinating area of study and speculation that requires a lot more research and one that will be, I suspect, revealing and rewarding for both these cosmic philosophies of life.

---

*For instance those by Sutin, Booth, Churton, Kaczynski, Lachman, Symonds, et al.

7

Paul Bowles

Expat Magic

Originally a lecture delivered at the Here to Go symposium in Trondheim, Norway, 2014.

ONE WONDERS WHAT makes certain people appear at the correct time-space intersections to make a maximum impact. It doesn't need to be loudmouthed enfants terribles forcing their way, nor fey, evanescent, and misunderstood geniuses generating emotional vacuums for others to fill. Some artists simply leave a trail of very tangible history behind them. And they attract both interesting people and events as they go.

It seems that conscious strategy is actually quite counterproductive in this sense. If you push too hard in the moment, you will be stuck there. You just need to *be*, and preferably be yourself, in the flow of things, in between events and key people. That in itself creates a resonant life rhythm, in which the beats are expressions and the syncopations the creative processes.

One such very rhythmically conscious figure in twentieth-century Western culture was the American author Paul Bowles (1910–99). His stern and elegant prose usually focuses on how people from one environment react in another. Bowles should have known, and did know about this, being a seasoned traveler and so-called expat for the greater part of his life. For him, being away from the United States was not merely escapism in order to find a nice secluded place to work. The place in itself—in his case predominantly Tangier in Morocco—soon became integrated not only in his writing but also in his general state of mind.

Initially Bowles's first love was music. He wanted to become a serious composer and worked hard to achieve that. He studied with Aaron Copland and traveled to Europe with him in the early 1930s, wrote music, and also had it performed successfully. He was at one point accepted by Prokofjev as a student but was too restless to pursue the invitation. Bowles wanted to be on his way, without really knowing what that way or journey would bring.

Bowles was in Paris in the midst of surrealism's glory days and was mentored by legendary art patron and collector Gertude Stein. It was actually Stein who suggested Bowles should go to Morocco in the first place, which he did, in 1931. Shortly before this he spent time in Berlin, where he also left his mark in his friendship with Christopher Isherwood. Remember Sally Bowles in *Farewell to Berlin* or its classic movie musical adaption, *Cabaret*? She was named after Paul Bowles.

He wrote music criticism for the *New York Herald Tribune* during the 1940s. The editor Virgil Thomson's strict orders were to describe what happened during the concert, *not* to relay one's own feelings: be sparse, economic, detached, but always eloquent. This clear and concise mode of expression spilled over into Bowles's novels and short stories.

He married another author, Jane Auer, and the couple became some kind of center of attention wherever they went. She was celebrated for her novel *Two Serious Ladies* (1943), and Bowles's reputation as a cultured composer and writer of reviews opened many doors in a postwar American environment ready for experimentation of all kinds.

The Bowleses traveled in Asia (where they even bought a small island outside Sri Lanka and then spent several months per year there), Central and South America, and Europe, but once they had established themselves somewhat in Tangier, it seemed impossible to leave. It was a cheap place to live, and its strategic position as an international free-trade zone brought interesting people, drugs, and sexualities. Under the surface it was indeed a liberal place. That is, if you were a Westerner with money to spend. Noël Coward once called the city "a sunny place for shady people."

Of course, the Bowleses were not alone here. Fellow expats with somewhat similar backgrounds were Brion Gysin, a close friend of Bowles's (they had met already in 1938 in Paris), and William Burroughs. Although these two beat mentors have contributed immensely to the glamour of Morocco, it was always Paul and Jane Bowles who were the real royalty. They weren't beat at all, but rather aloof yet welcoming to this newer generation of Ginsbergs, Kerouacs, and others. William Burroughs's paranoid "Interzone" environment was a drug-filtered version of 1950s and '60s expat Tangier. Tennessee Williams, Gore Vidal, Truman Capote, Cecil Beaton, Francis Bacon, and many other gay culturati flocked to the liberal city they had all heard so much about. And Paul Bowles was undoubtedly king of the hill.

Bowles's presence was actually the reason for Burroughs's coming to Tangier in the first place.[1] Burroughs often called Bowles's first novel, *The Sheltering Sky,* a "perfect" novel. When Burroughs originally arrived, though, Bowles was out of town, which made Burroughs critical and moody: "And don't ever fall for this inscrutable oriental shit like Bowles puts down (that shameless faker). They are just a gabby, gossipy simple-minded, lazy crew of citizens."[2] It took time before these two expats really met, and even then, it was slightly troublesome. Burroughs had borrowed a bound original script of Tennessee Williams's *The Angel in the Alcove* from Bowles. When he returned it, it was splattered with blood from Burroughs's shooting up heroin beside the manuscript.[3] Eventually, though, a friendship grew.

As the decades passed, Bowles became an icon of sorts, someone you sought out in Morocco if you were a budding writer or artist. Knowing Bowles opened doors, although he himself just existed in the here and now and never really networked actively in the way we think about it today. There seems to have existed some kind of aura around him and his work that attracted similar minds or at least wannabe similar minds looking for adventure, allowing the imagination to bloom, seeing other parts of the world, getting high and getting away.

Bowles continued writing until his death in 1999, always in the same style and usually on the same themes. After Black Sparrow Press anthologized his short stories in 1979 (a volume that was introduced by Gore Vidal), a new interest in his work emerged. Bernardo Bertolucci made a successful movie of *The Sheltering Sky* in 1990 with John Malkovich and Debra Winger, which brought new generations to Bowles's work.

As mentioned, Bowles died in 1999 and seemed not too distraught about moving on. On the whole, all through his life he seems to have been permeated by a real sense of detachment, a *désinvolture* not unlike that of German author Ernst Jünger. He was diligent in his writing and made very sure life swirled around the work, not the other way around.

There's no escaping that Bowles's work has one underlying theme: getting away—either getting away from somewhere or to somewhere, but also getting away *with* things that are immoral or downright criminal. There is no sense of traditional justice in his stories, and there isn't really any kind of deep-seated moral code involved. There's a pragmatism about life, a sense of seeing what is possible. I believe this was very much influenced by Moroccan culture in Bowles's case.

Expat is short for *ex patria:* "outside the fatherland or nation." This was of course true for Bowles. But it can also mean outside the sphere of the father, and this was equally important, consciously or not. Bowles hated his father and, as he often expressed, couldn't wait to get away. The young Bowles wasn't allowed to see other children, and his compensatory and creative mind started reading and writing and making up fantasy worlds, complete with maps and directions. Quite often, his father literally destroyed these fantasy worlds of the confused boy.

The imprint to rebel against authority and to be optimally free in mind and body was there already from the start. Music became the initial door opener for the young Bowles, and the 1920s in general was filled with a "Gershwinian" attitude of experimentation, mixing classical structures with jazz and other experimental approaches. It's no wonder that Bowles was attracted to this new wave of music: cosmopolitan, urban, free-spirited, open-minded, and playful. Clashing or contrasting elements temporarily set aside normal conventions and apprehensions, which in turn opened up the mind even more.

Although Bowles was never a literary experimentalist in the same way as he was with music, the themes and environments bring out the same elements. There's the known and unknown, the right and the wrong, the expected and the unexpected, always in dynamic relationship. But the prose is most often clear and concise and decidedly unemotional. Is that perhaps why it works so well in regard to describing the protagonists' often quite irrational behavior?

Paul Bowles was an expat magician not only in the sense of being an American in a different world. He also used elements of contrasting mind frames: Western/Eastern, Christian/Muslim, male/female, sober/stoned, and so on. And these were often placed in environments where you either have to adapt or perish, no matter how confusing the experience. He further tricked his own rational mind and its entrapments by being more or less constantly stoned on cannabis. Never zonked out of his mind but just enough to allow for a creative authorship to take charge of stifling "paternal" rationalism. So in many ways he sought out a creative liberation in mind and body, and this was also allowed to leak into his writings thematically and in terms of settings.

I have been touching upon "expat magic" as a process, a euphemism of sorts for a writer's need to displace him- or herself in the physical, outer world. But there's also something very much more tangible in Bowles's case, and that is his interest in the rituals and customs of the North African tribes, so different both in comparsion with "dark" Africa and Arab culture. The Maghrebi culture was (and perhaps still is) steeped in magic, curses, spells, rituals, talismans. Bowles first arrived at a time when the postcolonial attitudes among the locals tried their best to erase all magic. No such luck.

Bowles wrote about this everyday magic in many of his stories, and his ambitious project in 1959 of traveling around in Morocco to record tribal music and rituals is well documented and extremely fascinating.*

> Always without formulating the concept, I had based my sense of being in the world partly on an unreasoned conviction that certain areas of the earth's surface contained more magic than others. Had anyone asked me what I meant by magic, I would probably have defined the word by calling it a secret connection between the world of nature and the consciousness of man, a hidden but direct passage which bypassed the mind.[4]

One important function of art is creating a sense of "displacement": the more apart and displacing, the greater the effect. A negative reaction to, for instance, abstract art simply means fear of one's own personal displacement in general. To be a part of expat magic one needs to immerse oneself in something else, something different, the other, the unexpected. Just being in that state of mind creates synchronistically conducive effects.

Placing a fictional story in a different environment than one the

---

*This project was made possible through a grant from the Rockefeller Foundation, and the archive including all recordings is now housed in the U.S. Library of Congress. In 2016, the recordings were released in a CD box with an accompanying booklet by Dust to Digital.

reader knows creates a displacement, a suspension both of belief and disbelief, a setting free of the reader's mind. Placing yourself in a different environment while creating a work of fiction or art amplifies that process and feeds back. This is especially valid or potent when you blur or disintegrate the boundaries between the concepts of tourist and traveler (something Bowles wrote about and defined several times). The tourist takes in but returns. Everything will return to the casual balance of home. But the traveler goes on and never allows that return. This creates a more or less constant mind frame of displacement, one that can bring out entirely new ideas and emotions in the creative process, regardless of whether the ideas or emotions have to do with the specific geographical place or not. "The tourist accepts his own civilization without question; not so the traveler, who compares it with the others, and rejects those elements he finds not to his liking."[5] A wise platitude often expressed among travelers is the one where it's "good to have a goal but essentially it doesn't matter because in the end it's the journey itself that matters." It's not the dreamed of or dreamed up Holy Grail that will reveal the magical secrets but rather the determined quest to find it.

Of course this is not a prerequisite to make great art, or great magic. But there's something to be said of the willingness to expose oneself to the outer world, firsthand. The magician's magician of the twentieth century, Aleister Crowley, traveled extensively throughout his life, to learn about religions, philosophies, and magical practices firsthand. His output would not have been the same had he been stuck at his desk in Cambridge or London. He was a de facto expat meta-magician.

Both Crowley and Bowles had an uncanny ability to be at the most exciting right places at the right time, in terms of meeting interesting people. They were both in Berlin in 1931, for instance, Bowles to study musical composition with Aaron Copland and others, and Crowley to try to reboot Mandrake Press and exhibit his paintings. Bowles found Berlin to be mostly a "gigantic slum, a monstruous agglomeration of uninhabitable builidings,"[6] and also filled with swastikas. His most rewarding experience there was the friendship he had struck up with English author and fellow expat magician Christopher Isherwood.

At a dinner in London in 1949, Bowles met another British expat, Somerset Maugham. He was by far the most successful international author on the scene (meaning: gay, internationally inclined, and very productive/successful). Although Bowles, in his 1972 autobiography, *Without Stopping,* focuses mostly on the fact that Maugham had very small feet, he also mentions that he helped map out a five-week Moroccan trip for the mighty Maugham. Considering how distinct and well-known Maugham was in his role or character, and how successfully so, he must have made an impact on the literarily budding Bowles.

In 1938, Maugham published a slim volume called *Summing Up,* filled with thoughts about writers and writing:

It has been said that good prose should resemble the conversation of a well-bred man. Conversation is only possible when men's minds are free from pressing anxieties. Their lives must be reasonably secure and they must have no grave concern about their souls. They must attach importance to the refinements of civilization. They must value courtesy, they must pay attention to their persons (and have we not also been told that good prose should be like the clothes of a well-dressed man, appropriate but unobtrusive?), they must fear to bore, they must be neither flippant nor solemn, but always apt; and they must look upon "enthusiasm" with a critical glance.[7]

If this doesn't sound like a perfect modus operandi or program for Paul Bowles as an author, I don't know what would. And there are other sections in Maugham's little gem of a book that could perfectly sum up Bowles "after the fact," almost prophetically:

> The solipsist believes only in himself and his experience. He creates the world as a theatre of his activity, and the world he creates consists of himself and his thoughts and feelings; and beyond that nothing has being. . . . Life is a dream in which he creates the objects that come before him, a coherent and consistent dream, and when he ceases to dream, the world, with its beauty, its pain and sorrow and unimaginable variety, ceases to be.[8]

Well, Maugham would know. He was a prime example of an expat magician, allowing the Asian South Seas to drag him along into very deep recesses of the human mind and its social Darwinist twists and turns, and not unlike yet another expat (British-Polish) before him, Joseph Conrad. I can see a distinct heritage from both Maugham and Conrad in Bowles's work and general attitude.

In 1950 Bowles and Brion Gysin went together to Tangier. Bowles was now suddenly an international star because of the success of *The Sheltering Sky*, but Gysin was depressed and confused at the time. He had tried writing about Morocco in similar ways but never managed to have anything published. Gysin: "Much as Malaysia belongs to Maugham, Bowles's Morocco is his own. I went back to painting."[9]

The Sheltering Sky in many ways set the stage for the coming phase of Bowles's life. Although the American protagonist in the novel actually dies in Morocco (whereupon his wife seeks solace and comfort in other arms and other limbs), a fitting description of or term for Mr. and Mrs. Bowles's life in Morocco would be *succumbing.* They sucumbed to the culture, music, kif, lovers (men for Paul, women for Jane) but only so far as they could retain the diametrical energy. If you don't, according to my own analysis of Bowlesian logic, you succumb until you simply die and perish. You need to retain the charge by maintaining both poles.

Another aspect of this lies in Bowles's portrayal of Moroccan and also Arab culture. Today, it is a complete faux pas to describe different cultures from a point of view that contains your own value judgments— especially when derogatory. Paul Bowles couldn't care less—perhaps a sign of the times. In his classic travel writings anthologized in *Their Heads Are Green and Their Hands Are Blue* (1963) there are remarkable stories and descriptions that are not politically correct by today's standards but they are incredibly vibrant with life, humor, and spirit. Perhaps it's necessary to be somehwat personal to describe something in a convincing manner? Is there even such a thing as objective history writing? I suspect that Paul Bowles's description of environments and characters are actually more telling and revealing than any kind of social-anthropological study based in statistics-filtered objectivity. His writings truly take you there, wherever there is.

Bowles's quite conservative appearance and fear of dirt must also have been instrumental in augmenting this dynamic of in-betweenness and tension. Why else would this experienced traveler almost always choose destinations so diametrically unlike himself? "I relish the idea that in the night, all around me in my sleep, sorcery is burrowing its invisible tunnels in every direction, from thousands of senders to thousands of unsuspecting recipients. Spells are being cast, poison is running its course; souls are being dispossessed of parasitic pseudo-consciousness that lurk in the unguarded recess of the mind."[10]

Relevant to this phenomenon is the short story "The Wind at Beni Midar," originally published in 1962. The protagonist is a young soldier who actively dislikes the rituals and trance dances of the djinn-possessed local people, in which ecstatic bloodletting occurs. One day, while out looking for small game to shoot, he's so high on kif that he misplaces the gun he's borrowed and returns with a bad conscience. The owner of the gun actually finds it in the countryside but decides to pull a prank on his guilt-ridden friend. He hides the gun in his room, and then insists the kif-smoking protagonist ask a djinn to return the gun. Reluctantly he succumbs to this scheme and the gun is "miraculously" found in the room. There is a double humiliation in that he is mocked after this, for not understanding it was all a joke. The anger he feels makes him go to a local witch, who prepares a poison. The humiliating soldier dies, and the protagonist feels some kind of justice has been done.

The story is permeated by this kind of highly ambivalent attitude toward magic and folk customs, most of which predate Islam. In a way it's symptomatic of Bowles's own attitude but also in general of Morocco's, post colonialism. A pragmatic use of magic occurs whether one likes it or not. No matter how rational and "modern" one is, there is always the underlying fear that someone might actually have cursed you!

One could also extend the Moroccan view of the djinn to the way Bowles constructed his stories. The dramatis personae are like spirits he evokes to move destiny onward, each with his or her own function but seldom endowed with any deeper aspects of will or emotion.

> I'm not interested in characters when writing books. The characters—the actions I want were decided for them before they existed. For a given situation I need characters who will react the way I want them to react in that situation. . . . A character is what he does. I never have any idea what the character looks like, if he is tall or short, fat or thin. A character speaks and acts. That is the person. Apart from that he doesn't exist.[11]

Later on in his life, Bowles had seemingly become more rigid in his attitudes. Perhaps the gradual Westernization of Tangier and Morocco in general had affected his younger years' open-minded amazement and made him more prone to rational analysis. In the final documentary film about his life, *Let It Come Down,* he says things like "It's absurd that there should be supernatural powers, it's a rather mad concept";

and "Being in love is extremely abnormal"; and "The meaning of life is inevitable death."[12] This sounds more like crude existentialism than someone caught in an exotic and creative in-betweenness. Perhaps the maps of the outer world that he was so fascinated by as a youth gradually faded, and the travels that had broadened his mind for decades were now but memories to be sorted out? What seemed left was only the stripped and quite often problematic relationships between human individuals, albeit situated in exotic locations.

For all his colorful expat magic and his desire to stay detached, Bowles did return home eventually, literally and symbolically. Not only in the form of his ashes coming back to the family plot in the United States, but also in a more rational and intellectual approach to what he had once sought out. He was a privileged and esteemed artist, neither beatnik nor bestseller, whose integrity was perhaps too solidly based in his detached stance vis-à-vis American morals with regard to, for instance, homosexuality and the use of drugs. Paradoxically (or not) his active detachment contained an equally active attachment to his formative years as a boy: a boy who wasn't allowed to play with other children, who could read and write at age four, who loved maps, wrote violent stories, hated his father, and couldn't wait to get away. He succeeded in great style on all accounts, so perhaps it was only natural that the final resting place would be exactly where the journey began. A full circle. A full stop.

8

Tangible Evanescence

Originally published in the anthology
Booklore—A Passion for Books
(edited by Alcebiades Diniz Miguel & Jonas Ploeger,
Düsseldorf, Zagava, 2016).

It is a remarkable thing when books call out your name from the shelf. If you've read a book once, shouldn't that be enough? The experience is already there in your mind, evoking specific stories, characters, styles, and so on. But some works of literature keep on beckoning and calling, and you return to them to be amazed yet again. This is, I guess, what constitutes the character of a favorite book: one you simply have to return to, over and over again, without really consciously knowing why.

I have several of these titles on my shelves. But two volumes that always beckon loudly and to which I do occasionally return are Ernst Jünger's *On the Marble Cliffs* and Yukio Mishima's *Sun and Steel*. They are both slim volumes, yet tight and packed with both content and styles that are uniquely those of the authors. Between them, they contain so many similarities that I simply have to look at them in this particular context as one. Perhaps not as one book, but certainly as one experience. And so we begin by asking the question: Why?

Jünger's *On the Marble Cliffs* is a short tale about unrest and turmoil between opposing forces: one being traditional, rural, nature-inspired, and life-affirming, and the other being oppressive, violent, power soaked, and vaguely political. The protagonist, a former soldier, leads an almost monastic life in the service of a poetic approach to the natural sciences. The outer circumstances, with an approaching war and upheaval of order, seep into this harmony where he and his companion enthusiastically analyze and catalog the flora of the region:

> Soon we felt our energies increasing, and a new sureness possessed us. The word is both king and magician. Our high example we found in Linnæus, who went out into the unruly world of plants and animals with the word as his sceptre of state. And more wonderful than any sword-won empire, his power extends over the flowering fields and nameless insect hosts.[1]

Mishima's *Sun and Steel* is not a novel at all but rather a coherent anthology of pensées concerning the relationship between word and body. The author meanders intellectually about his own history and how he felt pressured to find a better balance between his intellectual side and his bodily one. This is basically filtered through a highly romanticized death wish stemming from early erotic imprints radiating from images of the pierced Saint Sebastian:

> Nothing gives the armed forces so much attraction as the fact that even the most trivial duty is ultimately an emanation of something far loftier and more glorious, and is linked, somewhere, with the idea of death. The man of letters, on the other hand, must scratch together his own glory from the rubbish within himself, already overfamiliar in every detail, and refurbish it for the public eye.[2]

The similarities thematically are obvious. There is, in both books, an awareness of temporal finality that is accepted as a fundament of existence. In Jünger's case, his attitude as a historian of sorts makes his characters go through the motions of resistance (although seemingly futile) simply because that's the way life works, and the only redeeming possibility is one of noble and elevated behavior. This in no way indicates moralism or religious fervor, though. It's simply a way of helping ideas and ideals to survive beyond the cataclysms that are already apparent and approaching.

Mishima is also, like Jünger, at war with the outside world. Postwar Japan and its rapid infusion of both Western capital and culture (and its ensuing decadence) made the budding writer a conservative force to be reckoned with. First as a writer and then gradually within his own little military society, which had sworn to be at the service of the recently emasculated emperor. In the intense training of his own body, Mishima not only prepared for new levels of awareness as a writer but also ultimately for his own suicide in 1970 (*Sun and Steel* was written just prior to his death). That this suicide should be seen as a sacrifice is obvious.

Mishima battles with the enigmatic force field between words as conveyors of morals and spiritual values and their equally seductive power to entertain, this process being very much extended to and in the public persona of Mishima himself. In this strange mix between aspiration, bodybuilding, and a romanticized death wish, *Sun and Steel* is like an intellectual tornado of both a highly refined (wished for) control and a desperation to overcome weakness in order to meet the inevitable on one's own terms. It is a way of cheating death, yes, but only by tricking it ahead of time through one's own design.

Jünger's protagonist—as is often the case, truly a reflection of the author's own persona—is aloof and reflective, yet not passive and escapist. His botanical studies contain fodder for haughty philosophical speculation and even catalysts for interpreting the threatening outside world. As with Mishima's own body, Jünger's lofty "naturalism" becomes both an extension of inner processes that eventually drift out *and* an entry into an even deeper potential introspection. When the protagonist leaves the sanctuary on the marble cliffs that contains all the remnants and collections of years of study and reflection, he makes sure to burn it to the ground—thereby making it a sacrifice rather than having it soiled by the approaching oppressive forces. Order, beauty, and life itself seem evanescent and temporal, but within certain limits we can decide how to begin, how to develop, and how to end it all. Again, it's a way of assuming slight control before the inevitable occurs.

These actions could of course be seen as vain, in vain, and illusory, but in both cases I can't see it quite so negatively. After all, Mishima did succeed in every aspect in achieving what he wanted and is today what he hoped to be: a symbol of a poetic and traditional resistance to the Western "nothingness" and consumerism that was already apparent in Japan (and elsewhere) right after the Second World War. Jünger was lucky to escape the Nazi "bureaucracy of death" and Goebbels's love-hate relationship with him. *On the Marble Cliffs* was published in 1939, and its criticism of totalitarian strategies, attitudes, and negative effects would have had any other author killed. According to contemporary Jünger mythos, he was basically saved or spared because Hitler himself liked Jünger as a type/character—impressions founded on Jünger's initial claim to literary fame, the First World War novel *The Storm of Steel* (1920).

Jünger himself classified *On the Marble Cliffs* as a general overview of the dynamics of tyranny and has stated that it wasn't specifically about Nazi Germany at all. Be that as it may, that angle of specific interpretation will of course always be there. Mishima is similarly elusive. His own paramilitary "Society of Shields" made no claims to oppose anything but the general morass of contemporary life and culture. Yet Japan had been one of the Axis powers fighting side by side with Nazi Germany, and even more adamantly so for several months after Germany had surrendered. In this we can find more similarities between the authors mainly, but also between these specific books.

Jünger refused to adapt or succumb to the new regime's "denazification" process simply because he had never been a Nazi. This of course initially led to problematic stigmatization for him in those truly dualistic times. It wasn't until 1947 that *On the Marble Cliffs* was published in an English translation (incidentally, made by a British officer, Stuart Hood, who had met Jünger right at the end of the war). For Mishima the situation was even stranger, as his pro-nationalistic ultraconservatism came much later, some twenty years after the end of the war. The romantic yearning for an idyllic society or era is fundamental in both books, but both authors seem aware that it's an evanescent pipe dream that can only truly exist in a constructed memory or within the unlimited world of fiction: "Anything that comes into our minds, even for the briefest of moments, exists. Even though it may not exist at the actual moment, it has existed somewhere in the past, or will exist at some time in the future."[3]

The pro-militaristic stance of the authors permeates both books. Jünger had indeed been a soldier in both world wars and was imbued early on with a chivalric Prussian attitude toward military life—one that never really left him. Mishima was a faint and fey aesthete during the war, and his pro-militaristic stance became part therapy and part mission much later on: "The thing that lay at the far end of my dreams was extreme danger and destruction; never once had I envisaged happiness. The most appropriate type of daily life for me was a day-by-day world destruction; peace was the most difficult and abnormal state to live in."[4] Where *On the Marble Cliffs* is a fairy tale–like allegory of cyclic history and chivalric resistance, *Sun and Steel* is a more concrete report of a similar process, albeit individual. Both authors positioned themselves outside contemporary concerns in almost anachronistic ways and relayed their philosophy through literature. What permeates both books is an elegant display not only of a personal approach (that could have ended with execution for Jünger and possibly prosecution for Mishima) but also of a deep conviction and love for literature as such. Jünger found his vocation in letters early on, as did Mishima. Jünger seemingly had no qualms about it—on the contrary, the audacity in his works is sometimes staggering and, to some, provocative. Mishima's doubts lay not so much in his qualities as an author but rather in the self-esteem that the public persona as author made obvious to him. Both of these short books show so clearly how evocative and thereby inspirational writing can be, regardless if it's a question of allegorical fiction or a call to arms in regard to personal weaknesses.

At the same time, both do battle with the very process of writing and storytelling itself. Mishima's struggle in *Sun and Steel* is an overcoming of the apparent contradiction of literary creation—at least his own. Hence, I assume, is the fact that it is not a novel at all but rather a straight recounting of his own call to arms—arms that were ideally to be part writing and part physical excellence in anticipation of death. Jünger experienced similar concerns. He knew all along that to be free one has to be outside of polarities and attachments. More and more, he refined the anarch's stance of being outside by integrating the fable's form as narrative and nature as such as the perfect allegorical platform for his various protagonists' voices. It is as if they both constantly evaluated not only story itself but also storytelling. The awareness of the dangers of verbiage, demagogic or not, was present in them both, but they seemingly had different approaches in this regard. Jünger drifted methodically into mythological evanescence and Mishima painstakingly into a physical one. Jünger wrote

> If I do not describe the details of our work it is because we were busied with things which lie beyond speech and which therefore elude the spell that words exert. But everyone will remember how his mind has labored in regions which he cannot portray, whether it were in dreams or in deep thought. It seemed as if he were groping for the right road in labyrinths or sought to unravel the figures among the patterns of an optical illusion. And often

he awoke wonderfully strengthened. That is where our best work takes place, and so it seemed to us, too, that in our struggle speech was still inadequate, and that we must penetrate into the depths of the dream if we were to withstand the threat against us.[5]

And Mishima: "The cynicism that regards all hero worship as comical is always shadowed by a sense of physical inferiority."[6]

Both gentlemen are balancing on a tightrope between free-spirited, amazing individual creativity and conservative demagogy. A little bit more (of anything) would have positioned them elsewhere, but this fine-tuned awareness, not only of personal approach but also of literary skill, instead place them as steady beacons in the reader's mind.

I had my hesitations about writing this short essay simply because I was afraid that the process of analysis would create a de-attraction to both books. Sometimes the magic should remain unquestioned and just enjoyed. But I still feel attracted to them, so no harm done. In this wild speculation of mine, what unites the books (and perhaps the authors themselves too) is the anachronistic outsider's advantage of being able to be free to create at will, undisturbed by temporal concerns or, even worse, literary styles or trends. Their force lies not so much in the themes written about as in the way they are written. They both contain a perfect blend of style and content that was truly unique not only to "their masters' voices" but also to the very lives they led. Perhaps one could call it all a highly enjoyable tangible evanescence?

To me, these authors, and these titles specifically, have been *very* inspiring. The meta-level of their language (extreme and literal in Mishima's case; alluded to in Jünger's) creates a totality that transcends mere fiction. Their existential positions as reflective anarch (Jünger) and active combatant (Mishima) in a world of utter complacency and existential nothingness fill me with the energy I need to evaluate which is the best attitude for me. As literature is so fully integrated in my life, the books I'm attracted to help me decide on the outlook of the day. These two beautiful gems have helped me many times to cope with the astounding stupidity of our contemporary times. So I guess it's no wonder that I keep returning to them again and again.

9

Anton LaVey,
Magical Innovator

*Originally a lecture delivered at Nekropolis Bogcafé
in Copenhagen, Denmark, 2013.*

ASSUMING THAT THERE IS already a fundamental knowledge of Satanism in this illustrious crowd, I'm going to allow myself to delve deeper into a few specialized sections of Anton LaVey's contribution to contemporary magical philosophy.

Let's generalize a bit and say that the first half of the twentieth century was all about synthesizing. East met West, and this was integrated into esoteric systems by intelligent structure makers. The Golden Dawn was one such group of structure makers. Theosophy under Blavatsky was another. Gurdjieff was another protagonist, and Steiner yet another. Aleister Crowley was perhaps the most well-known one. They all made nutritious stews but basically out of already existing ingredients.

The second half of the twentieth century was more violent and also more creative in many ways. As the recent structures had become established and their once-so-pioneering key people had become accepted teachers or gurus, a new breed bred on first-generation Thelema, Golden Dawn splinter groups, and assorted pre-1960s swamis from the East concocted their own syntheses and groups, taking, however, considerably more contemporary fodder into account than previously.

Science, psychology, irony and humor, art, speculative philosophies, and other previously rare phenomena within occultism suddenly overrode arcane concepts like invocation, banishing, Kabbalah, tarot, wands, astrology, mystical angelic languages and ancient demonic names, and so forth. Instead, the focus lay in spheres of experimentation, neurology, psychodrama, sexuality, and other nonsectarian core human phenomena. Old structures were dissolved in new ways of looking at things.

The Church of Satan was one of these precursors of radical change. Established in 1966 by Anton LaVey, the church's first phase up until the late 1970s was one of visibility and provocation. LaVey's colorful presence made both him and his church celebrities. As a well-formulated and intriguing antidote to the mellow and essentially selfless hippies of the era, LaVey was cabled all over the world into news and men's magazines, who found the naked women on his altar just shocking enough to print.

During the second phase, from the late 1970s and up until his death in 1997, LaVey became much more of a recluse and solitaire. He was established, and his *Satanic Bible* kept on selling and generated an income that meant he could thereby devote his time and energies to one of the key concepts of the Church of Satan: "indulgence instead of abstinence." One of the things he enjoyed and indulged in was writing.

Although his books *The Satanic Bible, The Satanic Rituals,* and *The Satanic Witch* are his most well-known, I would say that the later anthologies *The Devil's Notebook* and *Satan Speaks* are much more substantial when it comes to his own thinking. The *Bible* and the *Rituals* were basically assemblage volumes, in which pragmatically chosen material was edited together and augmented further by explanatory comments. But the two volumes of essays and maxims that followed much later, *The Devil's Notebook* and *Satan Speaks,* genuinely contain the essence of LaVey's latter-day wit and creativity.

The essays are also a great source of some groundbreaking magical concepts, both on the "lesser magic" level (willed manipulation of everyday life) and "greater magic" level (ritualized programming of a willed "Is to Be" situation or development).

Already in *The Satanic Bible*, LaVey had shown considerable creativity. Concepts like "psychic vampires" and the "balance factor" soon became household terms in America and the rest of the world. His description of the ritual space as an intellectual decompression chamber also hit home outside the strictly Satanic perimeters. As did the slightly later term *occultnik,* signifying a person who is lost within old structures of occultism without being able to see what's really of use on a practical, material level.

In *The Satanic Bible* we can also find an old-school method within occult writing: creative appropriation of an older source. In this case, LaVey's use of the Enochian keys originally written by Dee and Kelly via the biographer Meric Casaubon in 1659 and then regurgitated throughout the centuries up until Crowley. LaVey exchanged the final intonations traditionally translated as "the highest" with "Saitan," claiming the previous translations and vibrations had been erroneous. "The barbaric tonal qualities of this language give it a truly magical effect which cannot be described."[1] He also claimed that the nature of the scrying that Kelly as the "gazer" used had been mispresented as via the grace of angels, when in fact, according to LaVey, it has to do with ocular and psychic "angles," which can, metaphorically or not, open wide the Gates of Hell.

The Satanic Witch was a primer in applied, practical feminism. It also brought in concepts like the LaVey "personality synthesizer," or the personality clock. This is a method to be used in various kinds of matchmaking, human as well as within other areas of choice and resonance, not as a spiritual oracle of some kind, but as a down-to-earth method of applied psychology.

There was also the important concept of ECI, or erotic crystallization inertia, meaning that our very first defining erotic moments, like the first orgasm for instance, will be forever linked to the surroundings, emotional atmospheres, and so on, inside our psyche. That crystallizing moment will be with us forever and affect us all throughout life. As it is an overwhelmingly emotional moment, for good and bad, it can be tapped as a source of energy in magical workings. As with a general and honest definition of one's own sexuality, the conscious working with ECI brings several benefits to the magician.

One telling example most of us can see within our own culture is the fact that both men and women seem to get stuck, time-wise and looks-wise, in the period when they were most sexually active and attractive. LaVey pointed out some concrete situations where ECI is usually unconsciously used but even more visible. Solitary elderly people, like widows or widowers, usually become depressed and lacking in motivation. When in the company of people of the same generation, and in an environment that is created to evoke this sexual peak period of life, vitality and general health come back in almost miraculous ways. We'll return to this in the form of another LaVeyan construct: the total environment.

One important aspect of *The Satanic Witch* was the development of what LaVey called "the law of the forbidden," meaning that to attract a person or a desired situation, one needs to be genuinely aware of one's own qualities (this is very much tied in to "the balance factor" mentioned earlier) and the alluring display of sections of the body but *not* all of it. Showing a little bit of flesh by mistake can create a greater jolt and impact than quickly undressing and revealing it all. "Nothing is so fascinating as that which is not meant to be seen." There is even a chapter in *The Satanic Witch* called "The Secrets of Indecent Exposure." However, the dynamic need not be sexual at all.

The law of the forbidden can be used in many different areas.

Sexual honesty is paramount in the LaVeyan universe. Personal fetishes are also extremely important, whether sexual or emotional. To feel strongly about something that concerns no one else is to generate a force field that can be tapped indefinitely. To feel strongly about something that concerns a multitude of people is to generate leakage and distortion. To savor small items of active preference in a fetishistic way thereby becomes a highly conscious magical act. Emulation is *not* a key to Satanism. Passion, on the other hand, is.

What follows here is an overview of some further key concepts that can hopefully inspire the student to delve further into the mysteries of him- or herself via the Satanic grid.

INTEGRATION OF THE EGO

Almost all previous magical systems were developed within a dichotomy that was structured around the relationship between "higher" and "lower," no doubt having to do with monotheistic religious imprints in which this life is insufficient and that some kind of idealized pie in the sky is better.

The heavy influx of Freudian energy during the twentieth century revealed the power of the conscious ego. LaVey integrated the ego as a valid and relevant component in magical thought and thereby made void invisible moralisms that had up until then permeated the worldview of practically all previous magical conceptualists.

Higher/lower is in itself a concept imbued with value, and that value stems from control systems stressing that the ideal can essentially not be reached within the span of one human lifetime. LaVey, on the other hand, stressed that the uncertainty of karmic relations *possibly* transcending this lifetime is too strong, and that gratification of desires in the here and now is more of a natural given, and certainly more worth striving for.

One also has to take into consideration that will is always expressed through ego, and that even demigod characters projected with selfless, altruistic, and spiritual existence (the Dalai Lama, Gandhi, other Eastern figures, gurus, the pope, et al.) all make choices through their egos.

The LaVeyan perspective disrobes a great deal of hypocrisy in our zeitgeist, whether the proponents be political, religious, "magical," or just generally altruistic. There is always ego involved in decision making, and if this is not recognized and exposed, obstructing illusions will dominate the analytical faculties of those taking part. This illusion would only be deemed Satanically sanctioned if the person in question allows him- or herself to be duped in order to gratify his or her *own* masochistic need of servitude.

The LaVeyan magical system favors the eloquent will of the ego—as well as its underlying libidinal and compensatory forces—as the most relevant ideal to strive for. Whichever clothing this ideal is individually dressed in, it rids itself of the illusions stemming from other people's projections, as well as from *their* individual ego-based wills.

Although LaVey and later LaVeyans have expressed a critical stance in regard to a concept like "spiritual," the concept itself would be better off in a dichotomy called inner and outer (thereby leveling out or at least decimating any inherent value-based interpretations). We all work with processes of thinking, willing, feeling, and so forth, and they could all be seen as being inner and/or related to the workings of the mind. These processes are then expressed in the outer, filtered through the ego.

If the inner is inspired somehow by what is traditionally stamped as spiritual or higher (adherence to a certain technical language or certain techniques like yoga, meditation, or even specific religious thought or iconography) and this is expressed through a conscious ego, the ball game is moved from an externally controlled or imposed field of values to the highly magical and ego-gratifying field of well-being in resonance.

All altruism stems from decisions made by the ego, as does all non- or anti-altruism. This integration of a considerably more stripped attitude when it comes to the human psyche and its motivations is probably LaVey's most important contribution to magical thought.

THE VALIDATION AND INTEGRATION OF EMOTION

Where previous Western magical systems had been based on an intellectual and systematized/structured approach, Anton LaVey brought in the emotional as a key agent. No greater magical working can, according to LaVey, be successful without an evocation of relevant human emotions. Although this sounds simple enough, it becomes a dilemma when the individual is armed to his or her teeth with fancy elemental weapons and a perfect *intellectual* understanding of how to perform a traditional ritual. But what about "Why"? Why is this ritual performed? Usually, it's to "cause change to occur in conformity with will," to paraphrase Crowley. That's fair and fine enough, but if the magician in question works only within a strictly intellectual sphere with a rational approach, he or she might just as well focus on "lesser" magic, that is, a Machiavellian manipulation of the surroundings.

Any working dealing with "greater" aspects needs emotional investment in the ritual moment. LaVey's term for the temple space—the *intellectual decompression chamber*—pretty much sums it up. It is a challenge for most people to honestly know themselves and to have the courage, even in solitary settings, to display weaknesses and emotions not in line with the desired self-image. But how else can you develop, overcome, or banish these weaknesses?

A SENSE OF HUMOR

Of course, this was not invented by Anton LaVey. But few magicians have stressed it as an important quality and also a tool. "A Satanist without a sense of humor would be unbearable," he says in the documentary *Speak of the Devil*. The use of tricks, jokes, and pranks can be integrated in complex and highly serious magical workings, especially if it entails ridiculing a pretentious person or force or strategically demeaning or belittling oneself to gain a better perspective or position. The clown or the joker is indeed a powerful figure or type.

The Devil's Notebook is suitably dedicated to "the men, whoever they are, who invented the Whoopee Cushion, the Joy Buzzer, and the Sneeze-O-Bubble."

> Invariably, those with the most finely honed sense of humor find serious meaning in what everyone else ridicules. The very nature of the joke is its foundation of misfortune. The joke maker can spot the sham in acceptably serious situations. Then, having called attention to the deception, he may stand forth as a Satanic tribune. Not so easy is the reverse. The same rebel who defends the unpopular and the ridiculed, plays to an audience whose only illusion of strength lies in its ability to ridicule. It's interesting to observe how lower man, while realizing the sadness of clowns, seldom pays attention to them when they have serious thoughts to offer.[2]

Incidentally, the Satanically important character of the villain by his very antithetical stance also makes fun of the existing order and morals and hence functions as a liberating character—if intelligent and conscious about it. Scapegoating is an important and apparently necessary function in the human psyche, at least for egos that are not healthily gratified. To take on the persona of the villified or the mocking catalyst requires an inner strength not often found among the "herd," according to LaVey.

ARTIFICIAL HUMAN COMPANIONS

Inspired by his own misanthropy, nostalgia, and will to be in charge, LaVey early on started creating humanoid dolls, often as memories from his own youth. In the basement of his Black House in San Francisco (the house allegedly immortalized by the Eagles in their chartbusting song "Hotel California"), LaVey had a bar called the Den of Iniquity, complete with several artificial human companions. This environment and its denizens acted as an intellectual decompression chamber as much as the classic black temple space upstairs or the kitchen where he kept his vast collection of synthesizers and other musical instruments. To be able to make small talk with the drunks, the bartender and the old lady on the floor who was a drunken victim of LaVey's own sexual fetish—watching women piss their panties—became a sanctuary and a zone free of rational processes and expectations. Anything could happen. And often did.

The emergence of commercially available human companions (for instance those made by the company Real Doll) not solely intendend for sexual use is a clear current example of a LaVeyan concept manifesting outside of the strictly Satanic environment. (For more on this, please see chapter 11, "The Imaginative Libido.")

I have great respect for those who pioneer their own artificial human companion, crude as they might initially be. They will have come a small step closer to playing God and creating man or woman according to their desired image. With a creative outlet as cloaked in age-old taboo as this, innovation may now run rampant—more so than any artform man has yet known. The bizarre twilight world of the ventriloquist, the puppet-master and the dollmaker can perhaps be understood through other than the minds of psychologists. The acceptable schizoid element in all of us—the one that selects our mates—has a fresh, new, open portal to pass through. Through surrogates the race will survive.

Other comments from *The Devil's Notebook:* "the prime appeal of the humanoid lies in its approximation of the purchaser's 'other half.'. . . Artificial companions that are pleasingly heard, smelled and felt also constitute positive selling points. But that an artificial companion looks right is of primary importance."[3]

THE TOTAL ENVIRONMENT

One of the most important ideas or concepts along with that of artificial human companions is the total environment. Consistent in his exclusion of the herd that provokes deep misanthropy and his inclusion of personal esthetics and fetishism, LaVey's development of total environments are a key to understanding the subtleties of his magic.

In a world that becomes louder and louder and more and more fragmented, the existence of a sacred space filled with perfection and maximum personal resonance almost becomes a heretical act. It actually is. Not only does it affect you in beneficial ways like relaxation, excitement, and inspiration, but there's also the possibility of using these spaces (and times, if they are time- or era-specific) for creative magical rituals in many different ways and directions.

In *The Satanic Rituals,* LaVey stated that "Man's ugly habit of elevating himself by defaming others is an unfortunate phenomenon, yet apparently necessary to his emotional well-being."[4] With the development of total environments and many of his other concepts, there was no longer a need for LaVey to be a frustrated outsider in conflict with the herd. The Satanist's creative isolation in a space/time-warp-possible mind frame is one of silence and subtlety, and one of the greatest tools in the Satanic trade.

This, combined with honest self-knowledge and a proud appreciation of one's own kinks and complications makes for a good, solid Satanist. There's always a strong focus of real-life material success too.

But only based on the balance factor and what is actually possible for an individual in that position. Self-deceit is not a popular quality in LaVey's cosmos. "The most successful individuals throughout history have been the people who learn a few good tricks and apply them well, rather than those with a whole bag full who don't know which trick to pull out at the right time—or how to use it once they get it out!"[5]

The total environment encompasses many of the central LaVeyan concepts in one confined yet endless space. Personal preferences, aesthetics, the intellectual decomepression chamber, fetishism, misanthropy, and possibly artificial human companions to share the magic with—it's a sphere of clear-sighted yet romantic proto-creativity previously unheard of in "classical" magical lore.

INTEGRATION OF MUSIC

LaVey was a skilled musician and loved music. No wonder then that he had explored magical aspects of tone, vibrations, rhythms, the human voice, and all of these things put together. His own rituals often included his own playing suitable instruments. Sometimes the ritual itself *was* the actual playing of one selected piece of music with heavy emotional gusto.

> Music is the most effective tool for evocation, as the entire body rhythm is helplessly taken up by the pattern of life associated with the musical selection. A meaningful idea never dies, nor does the emotional response generated by certain compositions. If enough people are inspired or moved by these compositions, the selections become sonic repository for the accumulated emotions of all those affected by them. Becoming an all-encompassing sensing element to the collective feedback of a particular composition can yield a total evocation.[6]

Again, the integration of emotion is fundamentally important. There is probably no art form more emotional than music. To get into the mood of a specific working, the inclusion of a musical piece chosen for its evocative qualities is essential. If performed live, the emotional amplification will be even greater.

In discussing these things, LaVey also mentions "emotional chording." There seems, according to him, to exist one chord for each emotion. Animals respond to very few: basically pleasure and pain. "Humans have added certain chords to their internal lyre, such as sentiment, which sometimes appears as nostalgia—a combination of pleasure and pain. Humans' internal chording is more complex because humans experience a wider range of stimuli than do other animals (though, alas, the reverse is often true)."[7]

THE VILLAIN

Satan was defined by LaVey as a symbol with the powerful potential of accusing and revealing hypocrisy and double standards. Satire, irony, and scathing intelligence here become magical qualities, as personified in LaVeyan inspirations like Mark Twain, Ben Hecht, and H. L. Mencken. Wherever there is dogmatic hypocrisy and attempts at control through intimidation, there will be counterforces. When direct causal balancing is not possible, then a sardonic strike can do just as well.

In all cultures, the antihero, rebel, or villain is usually more popular than the (self-) righteous hero running the errands of the corrupt. Even worse than the hero him- or herself is the person cheering on the righteousness imposed by others. LaVey describes these people as those bearing a "good-guy badge." Gather two or more of these together, and an intolerant lynch mob is never far away.

The balancing force is the lone ranger—often a truly good and just person, but with methods and an intelligence in direct opposition to the status-quo behavior of the herd. "The more grandiose the villain, the more beneficient he is to society." And "The greater one's natural degree of nonconformity, the greater are one's magical powers."[8] This is no way automatically implies that nonconformers or outsiders are villainous or vice versa, but there's something in the isolation from the herd or the collective that is absolutely central in the LaVeyan Weltanschauung.

Besides the integrated sense of dark humor, there's also the concept of "noir" justice in both Satanic and criminal environments. The antihero of hard-boiled crime stories of the 1940s and '50s and his stern cinematic counterpart in films noirs often represents justice but very seldom the legal system. And the criminal world is truly one of Machiavellian strategies and the protonatural lex talionis that LaVey was such an avid advocate of.

THE THIRD SIDE

Oppositional transcendence is a fairly new construct in Western magical thought. Where Chinese Taoism has always favored the both/and rather than the either/or stance, Western occult philosophy has up until the twentieth century been bogged down by religious dualisms and simplified divisions.

Aleister Crowley was instrumental in this transcendental process with his famous definition "The Magick of Horus requires the passionate union of opposites." It is not only a "magical" way of solving problems or looking at things but also acknowledges modern scientific thought. Where opposites either clash or unite, there is a great amount of energy set free. For the magician aware of the mechanisms involved, the energy can easily be directed to do his or her bidding.

What's interesting here is what LaVey called the third side of any issue at hand. This side he described and defined as Satanic because it challenges dim-witted dualism. Reality is always more multifaceted than a yes or a no, and especially if one is on a pragmatic prowl for success and pleasure for oneself. Aligning oneself with either the "either" or the "or" is usually to take the safe way out. The third side may be controversial, but that's never a problem for a Satanist. "The third side can be the crackpot stuff of conspiracy theories, or it can be the most logical and simple, yet *deliberately neglected* conclusion."[9] In *Satan Speaks,* LaVey gives an example of how this dynamic could work as a pragmatic magical formula mixing two iconic almost mythic energies of twentieth-century life and culture: National Socialism and Judaism. LaVey himself was Jewish by birth and at times even expressed Zionist leanings, but at the same time he admired fascist aesthetics from both Italy and Nazi Germany.

> It will become easier and more convincing for any Satanist to combine a Jewish lineage with a Nazi aesthetic, and with pride rather than with guilt and misgiving. The die is cast with the vast numbers of children of mixed Jewish/Gentile origins. They need a place to go. They need a tough identity. They won't find it in the Christian church, nor will they find it in the synagogue. They certainly won't find acceptance among identity anti-Christian anti-Semites who use noble, rich, and inspirational Norse mythology as an excuse and vehicle to rant about the "ZOG." The only place a rational amalgam of proud, admitted Zionist Odinist Bolshevik Nazi Imperialist Socialist Fascism will be found—and championed—will be in the Church of Satan.[10]

Criticism of Anton LaVey and his genuinely creative concepts most often stem from blunt prejudice within the critic. When the individual feels safe and comfortable within a system, even systems of otherwise radical and provocative concepts, the critical faculties toward that system become void, and scapegoating toward others begin. While often being brushed off as a con man or a charlatan by these kinds of critics,

Anton LaVey still lingers on as an important player in contemporary magical philosophy. He was decidedly a heretic but perhaps not so much against the Christian Church and other monotheistic control systems (these being already increasingly redundant and far too easy to mock), but more so in relation to the magical moralists all too happy to do some unconscious scapegoating and all too happy to flaunt their degree-studded good-guy badges.

There are many other concepts that deserve a closer study: LaVey's thoughts on masochism in relation to beneficial slavery, the "law of the trapezoid," and "lycanthropic metamorphosis," to mention but a few. I hope this lecture has at least laid a solid base as an overview for future interest and attention. In closing, here are some final thoughts from LaVey:

> When I think of all those who would rejoice at my discomfort, I am energized and strengthened to the extent that I might overcome any malaise. It is not my love for mankind that sustains me, but rather mankind's resentment of me. My disdain and contempt for the mediocre masses in general and those who calumniate me in paticular angers me to regeneration.[11]

10

Carl Jung, Mythmaker

Originally a lecture delivered at Aniara
in Gothenburg, Sweden, 2016.

ON THE WHOLE, Carl Jung is already so well documented and well-known that it's almost not worth talking about him. Jung is a superstar of a different kind than Freud, despite the fact that they have both been important pioneers within psychology as we know it. The word *pioneer* isn't even enough to describe them. They are both rather founders of modern psychology, which has now, in its rebellious-teen independent phase, tossed them both out. Jung packed a stronger punch, but not because he was less esoteric and less incomprehensible than Freud—in many ways he was more so—but because he was taken in and integrated in the surrounding culture much faster.

Even early on Jung was part of culture. The Dada movement shared the same environment as the budding psychology movement in Switzerland. Hermann Hesse was his patient, he visited the Monte Verita commune at Ascona, and he had a creativity of his own that he desperately tried to come to terms with. Jung also interpreted cultural phenomena in more general ways than Freud, whose focus was usually on the individual and on isolated experiences. Jung focused considerably more on the integration and analysis of myths, religions, customs, and symbols.

In the development of concepts like "archetypes" and the "collective unconscious," Jung not only looked at isolated myths in themselves but also at their artistic expressions. He claimed that there is an impulse-generating layer in the psyche that is shared by all human beings and that can be directly accessed through introspection, dreams, the study of myths, and personal, artistic work. A certain culture can possess a more rational or "civilized" construction than another, but the basic psychological foundations are in essence the same globally. Jung's travels around the world and his collection of data confirmed his theories and became an important part of his system.

The general openness that followed after the Second World War—decidedly a necessary pendulum movement—was integrated in both Jung's life and work in an enormous amount of material telling the story of what had so far gone wrong. The individual's need to find him- or herself, a healthy individualism in a paranoid and collectivistic world, attractive myths with strong emotional resonances, the integration of one's own artistic process, and many other aspects eventually contributed to both a liberalization of Western culture in, for instance, the hippie movement—and later in what we today call the New Age movement—and perhaps even to a stronger presence of political liberalism.

One can feel and think what one wants about all of these manifestations but no one can deny the influence that Carl Jung has had on our culture. It's been there hand in hand with an overall need to find new ways that are not dictated from above or even from the outside but that must be discovered by each and everyone on the inside, in the spiritual and the occulted.

When things are broadened, popularized, and integrated in a culture, the precursors, pioneers, codifiers, and formulators are often lost along the way. Generalization becomes the norm, and old terms are used in new contexts in pragmatically simplified ways. What once originated in advanced psychological reasoning in an open-minded yet empirical method becomes vague sloganeering filtered through pecuniary potential. When there's money to be made, necessary hours on end on the analytical couch quickly become "success in just ten easy steps."

A pop-cultural book by Jung such as *Man and His Symbols* is filled with highly relevant material for a deeper understanding of *Homo sapiens* as a cultural being. But the main attraction lies in its accessibility and the opportunity to quickly get an attractive overview of the human psyche in an increasingly complex, confused, and fragmented world. One jumps over the conclusions and preferably also the demands of critical thinking to instead find an alluring and irrational solution to personal issues through a very general kind of inspiration. Where Jung claimed that many of our central myths told stories about essential things that each individual must process in a hard and quite often painful process of individuation, the modern interpretation, say from the 1960s and onward, has become one of facing the path of least resistance and adapting to its attractive shortcuts. Where Jung wanted to make us aware of what is already there, inside us, most people still keep looking for outside sources:

> I have called this wholeness that transcends consciousness the "self." The goal of the individuation process is the synthesis of the self. From another point of view the term "entelechy" might be preferable to "synthesis." There is an empirical reason why "entelechy" is, in certain conditions, more fitting: the symbols of wholeness frequently occur at the beginning of the individuation process, indeed they can often be observed in the first dreams of early infancy. This observation says much for the *a priori* existence of potential wholeness, and on this account the idea of *entelechy* instantly recommends itself. But insofar as the individuation process occurs, empirically speaking, as a synthesis, it looks, paradoxically enough, as if something already existent were being put together.[1]

One could definitely say that Jung is the contemporary norm in these spheres. His terminology rules, if not within clinical psychology, then definitely within popular culture with terms like *introvert, extrovert, synchronicity, anima, animus,* and so on.

Jung's integration of myths as an expression of fundamental psychological truths got a push forward through American mythologist Joseph Campbell's successful books, such as *The Masks of God, The Hero with a Thousand Faces,* and *The Power of Myth.* Here we also find an accessible focus on the analysis of myths, mainly filtered through religion, fiction, and popular culture throughout the millennia. Although social contexts constitute much of our lives, Jung and Campbell, as well as many other later Jungians, always stressed that development is an individual affair—that it could be no other way:

> It has been one of the really painful problems of the modern Western individual to gain release for his conscience from this Levantine assurance of a separation of spirit and nature (mythic dissociation), together with its correlative totalitarian dogma (social identification) of "society"—almost any quorum, it seems, will do: a "people," a "Church," even a trade union, or anything calling itself "the state"—as the only vehicle of value, through association with which an individual can achieve worth: when actually the truth is the other way around, that whatever human worth a social group may claim, it will have gained only by grace of the great and little individuals of its membership.[2]

In the 1960s, even structuralist philosophers like Roland Barthes began writing about contemporary times from a mythological perspective. He showed that phenomena like Greta Garbo, Einstein's brain, and even striptease must be interpreted in a mythological way. Like Jung, Barthes claimed that myth is essentially a language. Where Jung wrote that this language in itself also constituted an essential content for personal development, for Barthes the mythological language became more of a convenient tool for his own contemporary criticism.

But the very term *mythology* was brought forth again and no longer strictly within academic fields like the history of religions or anthropology. From a psychological perspective one could say the concept of myth was made conscious by Jung and his later interpreters. Suddenly it was around in a wider and more public context.

With this, the terms *myth* and *mythology* gained more meanings. Where the terms used to signify a group of behaviors and stories that had lived on orally or had been written down and could be focused on, today they have become diluted and can signify anything from a lie to a feeling: "No, that's not correct, it's just a myth," or "That felt totally mythical." This dilution is of course a part of contemporary Western culture in general. One could almost say that our contemporary mythologies to a large extent consist of upheavals. Not just of old kinds of tradition but also of how we experience them, how we value them. Perception certainly hasn't been sharpened (which some technophiles like to argue) but rather dulled, and the material we experience consists of impoverished and diluted versions of what once transmitted something substantial.

An example: Our Western dramaturgy is based on what's usually called a Homeric structure. It ties in to Homer's stories about Odysseus's travels toward distinct goals. During his travels Odysseus faces problems and challenges that he, either alone or with others, deals with and solves. This is a very simple setup and yet seemingly endlessly fascinating. The same story has been told in so many ways and in so many different media that it's mind-boggling when you think about it. The reason for this is very likely the actual weight of tradition. You tell your kids the same story that you were once told yourself. These stories are more important than most parents seem to understand.

But two main things have happened since the days of Jung:

technology-driven mass media is one, and the commercialization of shared public space the other. Both of these have contributed to the fact that the amount of fiction has increased in relation to one's own thinking. Where previously we chose fiction in a compartmentalized manner and actively took part in it, today we are overrun by TV, the Internet, movies, and commercials of all kinds, and this mainly happens passively. I have stated before (and I'll do it again) that we now live more in and through fiction than we do in so-called fact-based reality. Fiction has taken over. If we want to break it down one more level, we can say that our own mythologies need our voluntary submission to too much content, too many stories, and all too quickly. Unfortunately, that's when we leave the original function of myth—education, teaching, and explaining things that are conducive to one's own mental health—in favor of being driven into a wall of technological rule and perceptual deficiencies at an exponentially increasing speed.

How would Jung interpret our contemporary times? I can of course only speculate—and I gladly will. I believe he would have called it reversion. Where he claimed that the answers lie within ourselves on individual but also culturally integrated levels, and that one needs to work hard to reach these deeper levels, everything today is basically reversed or contrary: we encounter attractive tsunamis of empty promises in commodified and disposable identities together with fictions filled with immediate but evanescent saturation. And, to add insult to injury, these stories are told in narrative structures that "retardify" the partaker: we see what happens, then we see at least two participants retell what just happened as if we can't get it ourselves. It's a breaking down of the barriers of human intelligence and dignity.

The result is a kind of anti-Jungian abyss. Stress and existential anxiety increase and are not treated therapeutically, but pharmaceutically. The human being is allowed to believe in whatever she so desires but doesn't really believe in anything at all. And those who actually do believe in something seem willing to kill all those who don't share their specific belief.

If you simply exchange a cluster of well-tried and well-meaning myths for arbitrarily created (and often quite non-altruistic) pseudo-myths, then perhaps we simply can't handle it? The contact with the deeper layers of the psyche may actually be literally essential for the individual. That's what Jung claimed anyway. No outside structures can act as substantial substitutes for the gnostic and direct contact the individual needs in his or her development. One parallel example could be the fact that we can't survive if we can't or aren't allowed to dream.

One important part of functional myths is relevance. The reason why certain stories still live on is that they've transmitted definitive and engaging knowledge and wisdom. What is relevant today? And how should we preserve that in such a fragmented existence as ours? Very likely we're looking at oral transmission, possibly amplified by physical books. All the so-called digital storage media are highly ephemeral gadgets, and we all know it. They won't last. And what will actually be told? What's going to be relevant for those who come next?

Desperate attempts at contact with our own (hi)story and a permeating anxiety about the future are what's defining a good deal of our contemporary history writing. I recently re-watched the first *Planet of the Apes* films, and they are like a contemporary mythological gold mine, despite the fact that they are already forty to forty-five years old. At first, some humans led by Charlton Heston land on a planet that reveals itself as earth in the future. The planet is now run by intelligent, talking apes who keep the remaining human population as slaves. This is a simple science-fictional and mythological presentation: you travel in time to show a nightmare scenario. But the interesting thing about *Planet of the Apes* is that the story goes on. The reason for the power switch between apes and humans in the future is that some of the more benevolent apes in Heston's company actually go *back* in time on earth—as intelligent and talking apes—to an existence where they are caught and maltreated because they stir up a riot among the lower kinds of apes. However, their genetic offspring develop, take charge, and eventually enslave the humans. That is, until Charlton Heston shows up several thousands of years later. It's a very simple yet efficient time-warp–potential-loop scenario in which we are exposed to the problems of xenophobia, anthropocentrism, vanity, and the worship of technology in fairy-tale form. It is a beautiful and substantial myth. Similar examples exist in *Lord of the Rings,* which very much contains Tolkien's filtering of medieval European myths spiced with plenty of xenophobia.

Jung's friend and colleague, the Romanian historian of religions Mircea Eliade, basically shared and amplified his views: "An object or an act becomes real only insofar as it imitates or repeats an archetype. Thus, reality is acquired solely through repetition or participation; everything which lacks an exemplary model is 'meaningless,' i.e., it lacks reality."[3] The archetype is, as we know, a strictly Jungian term and concept. Archetypes are the forces or symbols that individuals can meet in the inner world, in dreams, visions, and in daydreams and that clearly reflect, if only symbolically, variants of current existential issues. This leads to the question: Do Eliade and Jung mean that those who haven't yet acknowledged the archetypes lack a sense of reality, or that they themselves are unreal? It's a highly relevant question for us today. If we are actively opposed by flamboyant superficiality and angst-ridden identity crises, then we can at most reflect each other: thin surfaces that reflect other thin surfaces. When this is passed on to new generations the result is an increasingly accentuated weakness.

Eliade also claimed that basically all relevant myths retell the original story of creation, regardless of which culture tells it. There is a need to be reborn, and one does that by acting out ritualized creations, or "active symbols" as Jung would call them. This is also interesting from our contemporary perspective: exactly which story of creation is permeating our culture and individual interpretations? Although it's tempting to answer "none," I think it's more interesting to look at one main current theme: active dissociation from the earth. In fiction, the threat has always come from beyond (the bend, outer space, another country, etc.). We create and enjoy life *here*, in our own little paradise. But as the threats of real life increase (terrorism, pathogeny, asteroids, etc.) and thereby disturb the smooth recreation stories in/of paradise, the current expressions (mythic or simply escapist) also reflect that increase. Hence we are flooded with stories of space dystopias (us going out, "them" coming in), supernatural creatures disrupting death (zombies, vampires, etc.), urban malaise, sexual confusion, more and more superheroes, and so forth. Entertainment not only reflects but also actively leads the way. Acclimatization to inner voices and spiritual helpers is regarded as a facet of insanity, while Pokémon Go takes off like wildfire.

We are permeated by an illusion of empowerment. One example could be the first Hobbit film. It's a distant part of a genuinely interesting work of Tolkien based on mythology. The first trilogy of film adaptations found a strong resonance with the zeitgeist and became an immense success. But in the first Hobbit film there are scenes that are distinctly plucked from another medium—that of the computer game. The dramaturgy, aesthetics, and experience transcends the story in itself to create a comfort zone in an abstracted tool or, as it's called today, a platform. It is storytelling without a real story. Is there any difference between that film scene where Legolas is jumping up and down on moving blocks and the one in the computer game? The difference is one of illusory empowerment: you can "be" the character in question in the game. It's like when children play: "I'll be this one and you be that one." The difference is that it's still a passive existence inside the computer game, without any connection to active imagination, daydreaming, associative fantasy, and so on. It's not a therapeutic process but rather just a dulling one. Hence it's not a myth but just mere escapism.

So how can we awaken the power of mythology if we believe, like Jung did, that it's beneficial for health and existence? Well, the mere study of myths is fascinating and rewarding. Jung can be hard to read at times, but there's no escaping that *Man and His Symbols* is a great introduction. Joseph Campbell too. Campbell created pop culture out of subjects previously reserved for academic specialists. In reading Jung, Campbell, and even Eliade we understand the weight and importance of mythology, which opens us up to looking at the world with new and wider eyes, and makes us connect even the smallest things with larger meanings. The fairy tale is the child's first contact with an abstracted world beyond the immediate family, and thereby a strong contribution to how one deals with one's own life later on. If, instead, you press an iPad or a cell phone with a blinking, buzzing game in the hands of a child to silence him or her, how will that turn out?

For Jung himself, being an ardent empirical scientist, it was difficult to open up to the inner visions he experienced early on in life. At times he even discarded them as "psychotic incidents." But gradually he trusted his own intuition and began work on the book that may be his most important: the "red" book, or *Liber Novus*. It was simply a book he wrote and illustrated for himself and which grew and grew with time. It contains religious writings, visions, and symbolic images all stemming from his own depths. We can't really say that Jung was a traditional Christian but he was most definitely a Gnostic. Many of his texts are Gnostic, in the sense of early Christian writings that claimed it was perfectly possible to maintain a direct contact with God without proxies like priests or churches. Jung didn't want *Liber Novus* to be published or even shown during his own lifetime, but when it eventually was, in 2009, it became obvious that the work on the book had been extremely influential for many of his thoughts and theories. And that he was actually a very talented visual artist too. It was during the work on this book that Jung developed his ideas on the collective unconscious, the sphere that he claimed all specimen of *Homo sapiens* share, like a general DNA of the soul, and to which you can return to access both information and inspiration in life.

> By far the most fruitful attempts, however, to find suitable symbolic expressions for the self were made by the Gnostics. Most of them—Valentinus and Basilides, for instance—were in reality theologians who, unlike the more orthodox ones, allowed themselves to be influenced in large measure by inner experience. They are therefore, like the alchemists, a veritable mine of information concerning all those natural symbols arising out of the repercussions of the Christian message. At the same time, their ideas compensate the asymmetry of God postulated by the doctrine of the *privatio boni,* exactly like those well-known modern tendencies of the unconscious to produce symbols of totality for bridging the gap between the conscious and the unconscious, which has widened dangerously to the point of universal disorientation.[4]

Unfortunately, I don't think Jung will reclaim his well-deserved central status within the field of psychology. Psychology is a phenomenon, just like history writing, that is at times too affected by its own environment and contemporary influence. But I do believe that Jung's thoughts and ideas will take on new forms and carry on within art, literature, and other expressions of culture. Because we don't really need more existential manuals or more neurochemistry, but rather intuitive incentives, in which we see the totality and our own story clearer, to be able to make our own decisions. Causal, empirical science just isn't good enough for that, so we need fairy tales, poems, and dreams, as well as old and new myths, to be able to act intelligently on both individual and species levels.

11

The Imaginative Libido

Originally published in the Polish magazine Trans/Wizje
(No. 4, 2013).

IT'S EASY TO SEE how dolls and playing with miniatures are attractive to children, whose imaginations are not yet repressed by the demands of adult behavior. However, the externalizations or projections onto talismanic objects are of great value also for the psychic hygiene and well-being of adults. It seems that the times are changing in favor of an integration of a wider definition of *play* and, as an extension of this, of artificial human companions.

The child who plays with miniatures is regarded as "normal." Indeed, the child seeks an externalization of fantasies in tangibly bestowing objects/proxies with magical life in a phase where confusion reigns and there's simply quite a lot to learn about how to behave and when, and so on. Traditionally, girls are equipped with dolls and household items, and boys with tools of various kinds (cars, weapons, machines, fellow soldiers, etc). Whether this is all tradition and a manifestation of imposed gender patterns from anxious parents or something completely natural, we will leave for another discussion.

Mimicking adults close by can of course be both good and bad, depending on what these adults do. At best, parents can serve as good examples of balanced and creative decision makers. At worst, their own

116

destructive behaviors can be contagiously transmitted into the psyche and behavior of the child in question. Using dolls in these formative years is a way to relate to and structure the chaotic aspects of childhood, both as amplification of positive emotions and experiences and as exorcism of bad ones.

Suffice to say here that dollhouses, garages, pastel-colored stables for cute unicorns, replica weapons, dress-up cutouts, grand landscapes with miniature trains and roads or even battlefields are integrated parts of growing up for most Western kids.

Dolls and toys in general have always existed and always will. Under dire straits, a stick and a pinecone can do the trick and get you to the "zone." In more well-to-do circumstances, advanced and expensive mechanical miniatures will help saturate the imagination. The value seems to not have to do with cost per se but rather with invested emotional and imaginative energy. Your own favorite teddy bear may not have been the most lavish, costly, or elegant but what does it matter? It was yours and you felt an intense emotional resonance with it. This dynamic relationship can be so strong that the mere thought of that teddy bear can evoke a feeling of warmth and nostalgia later on in life.

There are several wonderful museums for toys in the world. One of the best when it comes to dolls, teddy bears, and dollhouses exists in the old town in Basel, Switzerland. On well-visited floors are thousands of items, all beautifully preserved. It is almost like entering a shrine somehow, the way the dolls and other items are meticulously showcased and looking out at you from behind glass boundaries.

Not only is there an impressive display of technical craftsmanship (now probably lost forever) but also of the very essence of dolls and proxies; yes, they are dead but they can easily come to life (of sorts). This becomes especially evident when looking at the multitude of mechanical dolls and constructions that move, either wound up or electrically. Although their movements are likely to be jerky and stiff, the mere action itself does indeed tilt one's imagination. It is quite often an uneasy experience and one that provokes a light sense of fear. Probably that's because it mimics our own behavior or environment but in a disturbingly flawed way.

On display at the Basel museum are many dollhouses that provide an insight into the behavioral programming of nineteenth-century Switzerland (and, surely, other equally civilized regions of the world). Everything is orderly, all the boys and girls are well dressed and well behaved (at least on the surface and during opening hours) and there is an ample display of exquisite miniature items belonging in the spheres of home, school, and work. That this was not strictly a matter of toys for fun quickly becomes evident.

Technology and craftsmanship dictated the shape of these important learning platforms of the era in question. In Switzerland of the late nineteenth century, where 10 percent of the gross national product came from exports of mechanical music machines, it's no wonder that expertly constructed and fine mechanical worlds of wonder were presented to Swiss children.

Today, entertainment has taken over the same function. However, there is a big difference. Today, kids are educated in passive modes by a never-ending flow of entertainment. Where active fantasy and play-acting used to be key ingredients in the mental, moral, and emotional development of children, today there is a saddening prevalence of introverted staring into illuminated screens of varying sizes.

This is also why prefab household robots, for instance, can't fulfil the same needs as artificial human companions. Their robotic presets and cold, distinctly nonhuman behavior leaves very little for the imagination to work with.

The fear of dolls in general is called pediophobia, and constitutes part of a greater cluster of fears called automatonophobia. The considerably more enthusiastic attitudes toward the same phenomenon are called pediophilia and automatonophilia.

The eerie and sometimes even terrifying encounter with glassy-eyed porcelain dolls or even mute teddy bears, especially when one sees many of them at the same time, clearly distinguishes the thin line between death and magical life. By mere will, an inanimate object can go from being a scary zombie or voodoo horror-film-nightmare item to something that is "cute," "cuddly," and—not forgetting this—"mine." And then also integrated in harmonious playing, alone or together with friends. It's what the human imagination invests in the object that makes it come alive.

Historically, the projection of life onto or into inanimate objects belongs in magic and protoreligious spheres. Children have always played in this sense, but adults have also to a varying degree been allowed to do this. Rituals and ceremonies in all cultures have been creations by proxy, either for keeping a community together by sharing a belief system, or for making substantial and sympathetic changes in a willed direction. The use of totems, dolls, proxies, and so forth, has always been integrated in this process.

Imagination in itself shouldn't be forgotten either. This is a quality or essence that is so fundamentally human that when it is discouraged ("Stop daydreaming and get back to work!") it creates severe emotional imbalances in the individual. For children, using toys and acting/playing is considered natural. For adults, however, rigidity and obedience are encouraged. Interestingly, this is a process or projection that usually sets in as the individual becomes sexually mature. There seems to be a link in there somehow, one that demands that the two protohuman phenomena of sex and imagination should not be allowed in the same psychic sphere. Now, why is that?

There have been many pioneering psychologists and intellectuals who've focused on these phenomena, Jung being but one. His integration (not least in his own life and creativity) of the imagination and his trusting of his own intuition remain groundbreaking when looking back at the twentieth century. Several of his disciples have carried on researching this, including Marie-Louise von Franz:

> In a way, one must be potentially "whole" already in order to enter the drama; if one is not, one will learn to become so by painful experience. Active imagination is thus the most powerful tool in Jungian psychology for achieving wholeness—far more efficient than dream interpretation alone. . . . In contrast to the numerous existing techniques of passive imagination, active imagination is done alone, to which most people must overcome considerable resistance. It is a form of play, but a bloody serious one. . . . We also know that many alchemists used an *imaginatio vera et non phantastica* in their work, which was a form of active imagination. This gives us the satisfaction of knowing that we are dealing here not with a weird innovation, but with a human experience, which has been lived through before. It is actually a new form of one of the oldest forms of *religio,* in the sense of "giving careful consideration to the numinous powers."[1]

The American Satanist and philosopher Anton LaVey wrote and talked a lot about something he foresaw as a great business and phenomenon of the future: artificial human companions. What he meant by this was the integration in daily life of life-size dolls, with which you talk, hang out, or even have sex. LaVey himself had an entire room designed as a 1950s bar, complete with furniture, musical instruments, a bartender and life-size guests that he had built himself over the years. The possibility of venting anger or indulging in prurient fantasies (and behavior) in this strictly private sphere LaVey saw as something that could become not only psychologically healing but also a revolutionary big business.

Time has definitely caught up with this thinking. Where previously store mannequins were modified by a few pediophilic Galatea aficionados, now an entire industry has bloomed that makes life-size dolls, complete with natural-feeling skin, various hair- and eye-color options, racial features, and physical endowments. As with so many aspects of the development of human technology, sexual needs have been instrumental in this. Companies like the American outfit Real Doll manufacture dolls for sexual use, but they can of course equally well be used for polite conversation or whatever else floats your boat.

If you think it's strange that people of both sexes would indulge erotically with dolls or toys rather than with real people, think again. The predominantly female use of dildos has been with us since time immemorial and is perhaps the most common example of adult talismanic use in our contemporary culture. The use of a proxy penis not only gives sexual and sensual pleasure but also activates the adult imagination immediately. Also, try to remember what you yourself (God forbid!) or your friends did when you got a new doll in your hands. Wasn't Barbie more or less immediately defrocked and examined between her legs? Ditto with Ken? The curiosity and relationship has been there all along.

There is nowadays a gigantic global industry that has surpassed its cousin, pornography, and that is sex toys. That's right: "toys." And dolls constitute a large portion of this industry of adult toy making. Does this mean that adults have suddenly become more infantile? No, it very likely just means that the market now acknowledges a deep-rooted human need to act out fantasies in isolated spaces that allow for not only a sexual but also an overall psychic release.

As soon as you so desire, the pediophobic aspects of dolls in general are magically removed, and these become alive and someone you can talk to or integrate in your own and possibly your friends' interactions. That is, when *you* yourself make that happen by opening up *your* mind to a reality slightly less causal than the normal, waking adult state of mind. The doll then becomes very much alive. If it's only in your own mind or not is irrelevant. In the subjective sphere, subjectivity rules supreme. The pediophobic quickly turns into the pediophilic at the very first realization that you are now alone with your new artificial friend.

One usually says that size doesn't matter, but of course it does. Small dolls are for small humans, meaning children. But what happens when the dolls grow in size along with their owners? Well, they need to do what adults do, of course. Or what adults would like to do with other adults but for various reasons don't. The primitive inflatable dolls with washable plastic orifices or attached dildos have been an interesting part of human culture from the 1970s and onward. From a psychoanalytical perspective, it's very revealing. You fill a doll with your own breath (of life)—or perhaps use a pump—then fuck it or are fucked by it, clean up the mess, and eventually deflate it again. How is that for an analogy of the Western narcissistic libido and its shame-based repression?

With a new generation of life-size and life-like dolls designed for various purposes (basically with or without orifices), we are going to see a change in privately controlled psychic hygiene for adults. When Anton LaVey prophesied and in a pioneering way built his own best friends, he consciously and willingly paved the way for a potential quantum leap in human behavior:

I have great respect for those who pioneer their own artificial human companions, crude as they might initially be. They will have come a small step closer to playing God and creating man or woman according to their desired image. With a creative outlet as cloaked in age-old taboo as this, innovation may now run rampant—more so than any art form man has yet known.[2]

What the kids do with their dolls is their business. What the adults do with theirs, ditto. Those who can't, won't, or simply refuse to realize the potential of pediophilic power will eventually have to find themselves becoming unwilling puppets rather than (self-inflated) puppet masters. Interhuman communication is becoming more banal and strenuous with each day that passes, which is in part a result of intellectual depletion by technology. Why not rather live to the fullest and explore all the intimate facets of life together with a companion (or several) that is not terrifying and dead (nor banal and strenuous) but rather filled with exactly the kind of life and style you prefer and are stimulated by?

12

Formulating the Desired

Some Similarities between Ritual Magic and the Psychoanalytic Process

Originally a lecture delivered at the Psychoanalysis, Art, and the Occult symposium, London, England, 2016.

It seems to me that one is displaying no great trust in science if one cannot rely on it to accept and deal with any occult hypothesis that may turn out to be correct.

SIGMUND FREUD, "DREAMS AND THE OCCULT"[1]

IN A SPECIFICALLY WESTERN MIND FRAME, we can see many similarities between ritual magic and the psychoanalytic process. A lot of it has to do with formulation, lack of formulation, or, possibly, misapplied or misdirected formulation. We are creators of our own worlds, and they in turn create their own, on their own. Usually, for balanced individuals, the interaction between the formulating strata of the psyche and the formulated expressions is well adjusted. There are also many gray areas in which there is a discrepancy between the two. One such area is lying—or should we say"white lying"?—which could be seen as a minor offense of desired manipulation. Another more pathological area would be a phenomenon like Tourette's syndrome, in which there is a distinct lack of control of expression of key strata terms.

No matter which perspective we choose to regard this interaction from, there are analogies within the fascinating spheres of occultism and magic. I'd like to narrow that down to a specifically Western mind frame, meaning: fairly rational, decidedly intellectual, and to a great extent ego based. Different systems could be looked at here: Western ceremonial, chaos, witchcraft, and so forth. I'd also like to narrow it down to the individual perspective. What does the individual magician do or express? With this in mind, the equivalent of a white lie could, for instance, be a misdirected expression of will, meaning one that's *not* rooted in thought-through, individuated reasoning but something perhaps more immediate, ephemeral, or reactive. And the Tourette's angle could be the equivalent of magic as a lifestyle attribute rather than an essential, transforming tool that's perfectly valuable even though it's not visible and frequent on social media platforms.

Human language is both a blessing and a curse. Nowhere is this so apparent as when one is talking about oneself or expressing what one wants in ritual. Well, it's apparent in politics too, and in device-instruction manuals. The formulation seems to take place right after the need to express has encountered the comfort-zone filter, and substantial things are usually lost in this translation. It becomes a compromise that makes perfect sense to the ego, a signal filtered out with safe noise.

The destinations in terms of psychoanalysis and magical practice are basically one and the same: in order to change negative behavioral loops and hindrances, we gradually work on small steps and changes, very much through formulation, and hopefully learn more about ourselves while doing that. But in both cases, the road to insight is paved with eloquent defense mechanisms and delusions of grandeur. In both, the underlying problematic emotional or psychic cluster is protected by expressions of what *seems* to be will. That is, a desired direction.

But usually it is not ingrained existential will based on a 100 percent genuine honesty (if there is such a thing) but rather momentary bursts of what *appears* to be genuine will.

I am not a psychoanalyst but was in Freudian analysis for four and half years, five days a week. So if you're tired of my voice already now, try to imagine what it was like for me back then! Endless verbiage, swinging from low self-esteem to perfected hubris. But what gradually dawned, as it does, was the insight about the verbal mind's capacity to cheat in order to be safe, to be escapist in order to stay put, and to be intellectually alluring to stay emotionally remote. This insight was of great help in many ways, not least in the magical work, because I eventually realized that formulation is truly the key to development and success in this field too.

If I say something like, "It is my will to resolve this current problematic issue by changing these related things," which is what one often does early on in the magical career, as well as in psychoanalysis, this presupposes that I know, first, exactly what the issue consists of, and second, how the interrelated things are actually connected. But is this usually the case? I can answer only for myself and say that initially, I was very quick in both definition and formulation, meaning that I assumed that my formulations were based on insight and genuine will. Thereby I was very intellectual, specific, and causal in my approach. But I'd say that two-thirds of the time, in both ritual work and analysis, what was formulated was mere regurgitation of current affairs, frustrations, and haphazard attempts at solution rather than honest expressions of a deeper will to change myself, which would incorporate various causal changes in daily life. I wanted the world to spin around me, but that can only happen when I'm perfectly still and balanced.

Here is an example from both spheres. In magic, I wanted to boost a creative project to manifestation in a climactic ritual state of mind, and focused on that in a distinct mental-verbal expression, with high causal hopes. In analysis, I wanted to counteract then current topics of low self-esteem in relationships by becoming more extroverted and socially active in a quite forced way.

A wiser approach would have been, in the case of magic, to express this little specific need through a filter of much deeper resonance: "I want this project to be successfully manifested because that would give me a greater visibility in a field in which I honestly feel I belong on emotional levels." And in the case of analysis a better approach would of course be to *not* counteract but instead try to constantly get a deeper insight into why the low self-esteem was there in the first place, and resolve the issue. Basically, you can always go deeper and farther and when you do that in an honest way, the perfect solutions for minor issues will become evident.

In the Western sphere of occultism there is a concept called the holy guardian angel. It's integrated into many systems and often called by different names. This relates to a principle that is either a more elevated level of your own consciousness that guides you, or an external principle that guides you, depending on which cosmology you ascribe to, or subscribe to. Regardless of which main field we look at, it's an intelligent principle of externalization, not necessarily as a kind of mirror (as in the case of friends in a conversation which can evoke a "third mind" of creative epiphanies) but rather as an ideal that nudges you in intuitive, personal ways. It's like someone with a bigger picture not only of where you come from and where you are, but also of where you should be going based on who you truly are.

Does that ring a bell? In analysis, this would be the analyst who remains hidden, out of sight, and who, after an initial period of bonding, passive-aggressiveness, and transference, subtly hints or suggests where to go based on the level of sincerity of the horizontally positioned vertical aspirant.

This leads on to the question if it's at all possible to be alone in the process of self-knowledge? Do we all need a holy guardian angel and/ or a therapist? Of course we're all social animals with needs of different kinds of interaction; but what I mean is if it's at all possible to develop alone in spiritual, magical, or therapeutic contexts? Very likely it's not. Even the sternest gnostics and shamans need to contextualize, share information and insights, and compare the personal findings with those of others, to refine a process that is potentially endless.

One area that's usually at the attractive center of modern magical life, or the appreciation of modern magical life, is that of dreams. Magicians have tended to see dreams as prophetic or as a similar kind of interactive sphere as that of an inner core, as active imagination/daydreaming, as visions during scrying or astral travel, that is, as a considerably more active phase than the standard Freudian approach to dreams as reminders in symbol of unresolved issues. But the emphasis is there in both environments—a validation of a psychic sphere that demands a third of our lives, and which contains valuable information or fodder for development. We usually refer to the dream sphere as a magical one, meaning, I suspect, that it's devoid of mental, intellectual, and verbal shenanigans. Other, deeper forces are at play.

The complex symbolic language of ritual magic and occultism may be filtered down pictograms from dreams, passed down throughout the millennia. If we accept the interior interpretation of the holy guardian angel concept, including gradual accessibility to Gnostic wisdom, then all of the stuff comes from the psyches of our ancestors. Before the book form, and before formulated written language, it was easier to contain a lot within fewer symbols. Is that, perhaps, when the corruption and self-deceit began, that is, when we left the inherent meaning of pictograms or symbols in favor of abstracted letters? And is that the reason why many of them linger on in specifically magical spheres, that is, as a needed counterforce to the more recent mental particles of formulation?

From an analytic perspective this would make sense too. As we develop as individuals through anal and oral phases and close ties to the mother, formulation is actually what sets us free and makes us able to interact with more people than the mother. Spoken and then written language is what we use to construct identities apart from the merely biological ones. But it's a two-edged sword. Because if we have the power to define through formulation, we also have to power to cosmetically adjust and redefine ourselves in different contexts, like playing out daddy against mommy to please your immediate ego, or vice versa if that's what matters just then. The symbols of dreamland here become nonverbal soothsayers and truth sayers, and the pain of confrontation with certain dreams stands in parity with the degree of actual validity.

Freud's sexualization of human behavior, as compared to the more cosmic interpretation variant of Jung, also finds its expression in traditional ritual magic in the Western sense. We usually see ritualized behavior based in a dramaturgy that mimics male sexual expression: intellectual outset, transcendence into an encompassing energy, increasing frenzy, ecstatic upheaval with exclamation of more or less formulated desire, and a meditative aftermath in which the wand is laid to well-needed rest. Much of traditional ritual contains symbolic recreations of the original creation. Almost like playacting a Genesis or big bang for personal purposes. This can be expressed in inner preparations through invocations or evocations of third-party helpers, or in outer mapping of complex yet conducive symbologies (astrological, elemental, planetary, etc.) where the magician becomes a seed sower for a specific goal.

One problem with this dramaturgy as well as with Western systems and traditions is that they're all alluring, complicated, challenging, and mentally strenuous—which means "perfect" to the Western psyche. This goes for both ritual magic and psychoanalysis. Where there's a system that requires method, devotion, knowledge, and a lot of time (and in the case of analysis, a lot of money), you go to master it, with the causal hope of receiving a degree, a funny hat, or a declaration of good mental health at the end of the process tunnel. But still, the system in itself is not the refining or magical matrix. The gradual waking up to self-deceit is.

Freud's schematic model of the psyche stems from a hierarchical cultural tradition, in which the motivating desires and drives are "sub" conscious and that which guides us is "above" us. This is a prevalent model for most of human life and not even specifically based in a Western sphere. It's thereby no surprise that causal, hierarchical models appear in ritual magic contexts too. Whether in group settings in elaborate temples or solitary workings in the mind, there is the magician at the top, commanding the sub-forces via the centered consciousness of formulation. Even angelic beings within a romanticized pseudoreligious context are commanded by words of power and elaborate symbolic structures of correspondences in time and space. The more complex it becomes, the more complex it becomes. If the formulation of the will isn't founded in genuine self-knowledge, things can easily get topsy-turvy. Because a human drive is always stronger than a human intellectual concept or structure. Externalized dualistic concepts with projected or invested moral qualities can absolutely bite back if what you exclaim doesn't resonate with your own *genuine* morals.

In a more analytical language, you could say that that striking out in compensation or projection may not resolve the issues at all. It very likely will not. What's needed is self-reflection and soul stripping in a chamber with different kinds of reflective surfaces; many of them will be symbolic. If you're diligent and honest, all mirrors will crack and there will be no more self-images to see because you have become the sole soul-seer. That's also the result of the magical process. You may have wallowed through endless systems and initiations (and related power trips) but when push comes to shove comes to compensatory quaquaversalism comes to final stillness—hopefully!—there is only one unique and noise-free mind that is resonant with all other minds. On that level, a brand new magic is available, with no hocus-pocus needed whatsoever.

My advice both in terms of ritual magic and analysis is to dig deeper before something is eventually expressed in an intellectual decompression chamber that allows for things to manifest. The causal manifestation of something desired is totally fine as the cherry on top, but the cake as such is usually baked with considerably more complex and not seldom painful ingredients. That goes for both these areas. If you strive for the cherry but can't properly make a great chocolate cake first, you may instead end up with steak-and-kidney pie, and ensuing disappointment.

13

Zine und Zeit

Originally published in The Fenris Wolf,
nos. 1–3 (2011).

TRANSMISSIONS OF ESOTERIC KNOWLEDGE have been handed down to us over the centuries in basically two fundamental ways: orally and in written/printed form. As for the oral transmissions, it's usually in their very nature to be secret and secretive. One could argue that general-educational wisdom (stuff having to do with raising children, for instance, and conveying ethical codes) has been transmitted orally through multiple generations without these demands of secrecy, but it's equally true nowadays that even these invaluable everyday pieces of wisdom can be found in printed form. Or on the Internet. That doesn't mean they become more tangible and applicable, though. General human behavior codes simply seem best transmitted orally.

As for specific, "real" magical knowledge, I would say there are absolutely strains and lines of wisdom that continue to be passed on— and who knows where they originally came from. I have encountered reliable "witnesses" possessing such knowledge, and I have myself been given some teachings from nonwriting magicians that I know for sure don't exist in any duplicated form. Given their secret nature, I will leave those oral aspects right here. If you want eso-exoteric blabbermouths, please consult the Internet.

In terms of the written and in various ways duplicated word, it's literally easier to look at, and especially when it's "close to home." I think many of us share similar sparkplugs in our esoteric engines: magical books would probably be the most common one, that is, books that either have a strong evocative potential or books actually dealing with magical subjects, or else a mix of these aspects. We hear of things, we read things, we investigate and become inspired. And then we read some more. The books can in themselves become genuine totemistic objects too, if there has been a substantial charge of inspirational-emotional energy in the reading process. This charge can last a lifetime (and possibly longer) and can also be fetishistically enhanced by, for instance, an autograph by the writer in question, or knowing that the book has previously been in the hands of someone important.

The esoteric journal or anthology containing various minds becomes a multifaceted gemstone, with condensed expressions of human thought. The market in general is swamped by a plethora of books containing all sorts of compensatory epiphanies and claims of revealing the inner mysteries of both this and that (thank heavens book covers pretty much correspond to the contents—it saves a lot of precious time!). But the journal, be it occult or not, has the potential of at least displaying one or two facets one can resonate with, be inspired by, and, if one is lucky, allow to be integrated into one's own usable wisdom. It's a format that awakens curiosity and encourages taking a stand, pro or contra. It's a format that awakens further interest and makes you think and reflect. One crappy page of a book can be a reader killer. If you happen to find one in an anthology, just flip to the next article.

Thoughts like these were going through my mind while originally working on the first three issues of the *Fenris Wolf* between 1989 and 1993. Essentially, my goal was to collect the writings of the people I had more or less access to at the time, and/or that I had been inspired by. "What has inspired me will very likely inspire others too." This is a fundamental link in the chain of the history of human ideas. Stuff that doesn't really work will of necessity be discarded. Powerful ideas and energies will be cared for and nurtured and passed on, perhaps even slightly improved. I'd say that this is one of the reasons why the history of persecuted ideas is so endlessly fascinating. If someone is willing to kill you because you have a dissenting idea in your mind, you can rest assured it's a good and vital idea. Many of the occult teachings and ideas have been occult for a very good reason: self-preservation. But when the time is right, the flower in question will eventually bloom.

Also, there is one very substantial thing that I learned while working with various music fanzines earlier on: the world is malleable to a greater extent than what we're raised to believe—another very important magical insight. It's not impossible to penetrate new environments or cause change to occur in "conformity with will." It's not impossible to ask someone for something. Actually, my experience tells me that the answers to my requests have been affirmative and supportive more often than not.

These two aspects—a will to relay/transmit and a realization that it is actually possible—became the cornerstones of my youthful folly in the wonderful worlds of garage rock, sleazy films, experimental art, and worn-out antiheroes. Chat and snap, cut and paste (I mean that literally), print or Xerox, and distribute yourself (again, literally) at concerts and record stores. Very primitive stuff, but it worked. In fact it worked very well, and for each new issue, more doors opened. In my mind, there was already a formulation that what I was doing was magical in that sexy, supra-causal sense. As I drifted more and more into the hocus-pocus quagmire, my first priority was not to secure a gallant robe or an extravagant wand to zap the cosmic forces. No, the first priority was to create an occult fanzine, through which I could weave my own magical spells. If you haven't guessed it already, it was the birth of *The Fenris Wolf.*

Have you been aroused by a blog lately? I'm sorry to say I haven't.

I don't think I ever have, come to think of it. But when I flip through old issues of *Chaos International, Starfire, Nuit-Isis,* the *Cloven Hoof,* the *Black Flame,* old TOPY newsletters and fanzines, or the *Cincinatti Journal of Ceremonial Magic,* I can feel a tingle that is sometimes decidedly more sexual than cerebral. Why is this? It's because the tiny magazine or fanzine in question has been charged with intellectual or magical energy, best summarized as a will to share radical, substantial human thought from a unique vantage point. This energy sort of radiates from the pages, no matter how poorly printed they are. I hope the first three numbers of *Fenris Wolf* emit that same goodwill (some would say complete evil will). I think they do, but I'm probably too partial.

The return of the book-book is apparent these days, no doubt a backlash against digiculture, e-books, and toilet-paper paperbacks. For more on magical aspects of bibliophilia in relation to the grimoire tradition, please read Peter Grey's excellent piece in the fourth issue of *The Fenris Wolf,* "Barbarians at the Gates." It really goes without saying, but I feel compelled to say it again: tangible quality will last. Ephemeral digi-snippets of the contemporary will not last. If you want to share something and make some kind of impact while doing it, share it either straight (live) into people's hearts and minds or in tangible, multidimensional forms. So far, the printed book has proven itself a worthy winner in this regard. I strongly suspect this will remain so for a long, long time.

And when this long, long time has passed, I suspect that the impression of our own written magical transmissions will be a fragmented jumble of disparate expressions, each with distinct suggestions on how to cope with an array of problems and challenges—that is, a more or less exact reflection of the times we were living in then (now), albeit garbed in esoteric lingo.

I think the historic hocus-pocus traces will be obvious (in many ways, they already are). In or about the mid-1970s, a mere decade after the Aquarian psychedelic big bang, a huge release of creative energy settled in while we were (re-)evaluating those historic traces. Some have since preferred the conservative, museal, and cerebral approaches, while others have embraced a more anarchic, intuitive one, and then a zillion other approaches on top of that. However, what unites all serious expressions is that they will be regarded as serious down the line too.

One group or splinter fragment can't tell the entire story, as historians so well know. The more parts we have from the same totality, the bigger the picture, of course. Firsthand sources have a tendency to die, but secondhand ones have so far lived on for thousands of years, through the blessings of diligent monks (and others who could write and duplicate texts) and primitive printing presses. The more firsthand experiences that will be correctly documented and relayed, the clearer the overall picture. And here's exactly where will-fueled initiatives like magical publications, be they "order-biased" or not, have a huge advantage over academic writing, as they not only can but rather inherently insist on expressing emotion and wonder as well as mere chronological, factual accounts and further bibliographic references. That holistic dynamic of enchantment is required to fully "get" the picture. History as such, esoteric or otherwise, is never objective in its creation.

If a piece of writing doesn't express some sort of subjective emotionality or a distinctly personal experience, we have to cock an eye at its validity as historic "meme." If there's a too chronological or too distanced an approach, we can be certain that there's been an adjusted editorial process in action, usually in the name of objectivity. A peer review can just as easily be spelled *peer pressure*. And this, paradoxical as it may sound, is of course always biased and partial.

Don't forget that the biggest chunk of the word *history* is *story*. The more subjective stories we have, the better we can create our own synthesis, our own individual *Gesamt*-evaluation.

Magical experimentation in various fields of natural sciences, arts, music, literature, and so forth have later on become fundaments of "established" dogma in these fields. Perhaps what we have to consciously take into account now is the importance of "scripting" the future through various magical publications and shared efforts. Some aspects of science seem to be catching up a bit, but the magical sciences will always be way ahead when it comes to human potential research. I believe that all of the idealistic fanzines and small publications from these past decades will later on be looked upon as seeds, as sperm, waiting and waiting to fertilize some human mind-womb of the future. The ejaculatory process is swift and violent; human development not quite so.

I can sense (vague, I know, but deliberately so) that there has been an increase in occult diplomacy during the past decade, circa 2000 to 2010. This has, according to me, very much taken place through an energy-level increase in periodicals, books, and human interaction (symposia, conferences, festivals, and so on, not forgetting the integration of esoteric subjects and courses within academia, which has been a great step forward).

The Internet hasn't really turned out to be a garden of occult wisdom (not the same as information), but has certainly become useful as an extended address book and PR tool. Traces of the networking and sharing of resources, as experimented with in Thee Temple ov Psychick Youth in the 1980s, for instance, shifted shape and did indeed become a digitized storehouse of potential, albeit still dressed in the emperor's new clothes. The exchange of pompous, Masonic-looking certificates of mutual recognition has been replaced by a more thorough exchange of substantial information on grassroots levels, a merging of minds through tangible means, and a pragmatic occasional union based on tolerance. If the general objective is to further the individual in her attempts at elevation, of necessity tied in with a larger planetary need for survival strategies, then sectarian approaches and retentive affiliations might not be the best idea. Am I deluded when I claim that a new wave of occult publishers has been very instrumental in this Mercurial greasing process?

If Aleister Crowley hadn't worked so hard on publishing his occult writings in good, solid editions, he would very likely have been remembered merely through references from the gutter press of his time—like a vilified footnote in the history of British debauchery. Crowley's ambitious efforts not only at writing but also at publishing his thoughts and ideas, and his Herculean labor of hustling copies (truly the "Great Work" for us all!), in many ways constitute the foundation of the extremely vital journal- and book-publishing environment we enjoy at the beginning of the twenty-first century, and which, in turn, will help change minds, perceptions, and cultures now and in the future to a much greater extent than, I suspect, Crowley could ever foresee.

And let's not forget the magnificent entertainment aspect of occult publications. Idealism really is a lovely thing. There doesn't need to be a conflict between substance and lack of distance. No arena of human endeavor has been more touched by divine(?) madness than occultism. Delusions of grandeur in unchecked contexts create a splendidly entertaining stratification process. But when it's only spewed out in ugly and eye-draining Internet fora, who really cares? I see a very bright future for printed matter containing idealistic expressions, and one of many reasons for that view is that it takes real effort and real knowledge to create something that others want to touch and be touched by. Immediacy and complacency are usually very snug bedfellows.

Within this spectrum of efforts, there is one very usable common denominator that is also one of the cornerstones of magical practice: you use what you have and you use it to the maximum. You can't use more than you have in magic. If you're deluded and think that you can, it will very soon be made clear that you can't. Ritual magic and its synchronistically sparkling mind-universe isn't a credit-based economy. You are what you are and you have what you have. If you can play with that, it's likely that you can change certain things for the better. That mere potential of change is of course also exactly what attracts the Napoleon-Cleopatra contingent of "spiritual" loonies, that is, those without a solid firmament of substantial self-knowledge. But today they are more likely to ramrod online than to make books and magazines that require hard work and slightly more than an imagined crowd of admirers.

Looking back at the post-punk era and its spontaneous expressions, we find that the ones that have lasted, in the sense of still having a tangible presence, are those with a genuine will to express something, and then an intelligence to express and shape that into a form that speaks to its desired audience. As we're mainly book nerds here on these pages, I will leave the immense spectrum of music. Suffice to say that the DIY ethic, from the 1960s and onward (and with a particularly forceful impetus in the late 1970s), has created a great many cottage industries producing truly unique musical works, packages, products, concerts, and so forth. Most of these instigators used what they had access to and nothing more. "Where there's a will, there's a way." Is there a lesson here, why those products today (usually) fetch a higher secondhand price than a "top-ten chartbuster" that was issued in a gazillion copies? Of course there is. And the same goes for books, periodicals, and artworks.

Many thousands of years ago, the proper development of papyrus (Egyptian water reed) enabled a more elaborate and extensive writing process. A focus on religious and magical topics in writing was of course prevalent all over the Mediterranean hotbed of philosophy and spiritual speculation. The esoteric transmission may still have been oral, but as the Christian tyranny grew in fervor and indiscriminately killed off philosophers and burned manuscripts, the need for duplication and documentation became painfully obvious. The symbol of Alexandria's library burning (possibly the most vile act of terrorism ever) is relevant in the history of magical writing.

And then, there was . . . Well, I think you know that story quite well. And perhaps it's more interesting to start thinking about the future, now that we can safely study how the history of human ideas and creativity has been so eminently safeguarded by many wise women and men of various shades and shapes. Is it perhaps now our turn to face the future and leave something inspirational behind?

The magico-existentialist punches remain the same: Who are you? What do you have? What do you want to express? Find out in a genuinely honest way and you're halfway there already. As for the future: script it and script it well!

14

The Mega Golem Is Alive and Well

Originally published in the Canadian magazine Pillars *(forthcoming, 2018).*

A man and a woman were hanging round each other's necks. Nearer and nearer drew the corybantic throng; louder and louder the sound of the shouting. But my brace of revellers had turned now into one single form, half male, half female—a hermaphrodite, seated on a throne of pearl. On its head was a crown of a bright red wood, on which the Worm of Destruction had gnawed mysterious runic figures. Pattering blindly behind came a flock of miniature sheep, in a cloud of dust—perambulating provender that the strange apparition trailed in its wake to feed its train of dancing dervishes.

GUSTAV MEYRINK, *THE GOLEM*[1]

ONCE UPON A TIME, as my loathing for the art-world subspecies phenomenon "curator" grew and grew, I philosophized a lot about the nature of art. Is it at all possible to define what art is or means? If possible, for whom would such a definition be beneficial?

The more I thought about it, the closer I got to the very roots of human culture. Initially, art was tied in with magic, which was tied in with life itself. "Instigating magical change through aestheticized personal expression, thereby enhancing the experience of life" was the closest I could get in my own definition. Whether this just rang true as a justification for my own disdain for soulless, postmodern, intellectual art or actually works as a general definition, I don't know. But it made me think of the possibilities involved. So much (basically all) of primordial art consists of integrated talismanic essence. If art needs to be magical to be art and magic always inherently expresses itself through art, then it's just a matter of being (sub)conscious in the execution, isn't it?

The classic concept of the golem arose from the depths as I first actually associated the word *talismanic* with jewelry, smaller objects, sigils on surfaces, and so on. But the grand scale, in which externalized forces actually come alive and move about, is sometimes more alluring than the miniature world. Another aspect intruded: tangibility versus intangibility. Where so much of contemporary art is produced in order to be not only tangible and visible but also commodified in adaptation to a market, wouldn't it be interesting to create art that is intangible and invisible? And that despite this moves about and manifests change?

I remember vividly how greatly I was affected by Gustav Meyrink's classic "more Poe than Poe" novel *The Golem* in my youth. And that film trilogy by Paul Wegener and Henrik Galeen from the 1910s (*The Golem: Monster of Fate, The Golem and the Dancing Girl,* and *The Golem: How He Came into the World*) was truly mindboggling stuff that helped solidify a romanticized pop notion of what a magical golem being is, and totally on par with Dr. Frankenstein's more well-known creation.

But Meyrink's book contains deep implications beyond the merely "fantastic." Integrated in a fairly muddled narrative are facets of dreamscapes, multiple (or should we say interchangeable?) personalities, upheaval of linear time, reverence for the hermaphroditic, and distinct magical thinking. The golem itself thereby becomes more than a feared mythological projection in history, and instead becomes a representation of a dynamic human psyche outside the confines of order and waking, rational rigidity—which is basically what art should be a projection out of/from—at least under the umbrella of my own, above-mentioned definition. I realized that I wanted to create a soulful "mega golem" as a counterforce to postmodern intellectualism and commodified, tangible surfaces.

> I have given the subject much thought, and the nearest I can get to the truth of it seems to be this: that once in every generation a spiritual disturbance zig-zags, like a flash of lightning, right through the Ghetto, taking possession of the souls of the living to some end we know not of, and rising in the form of a wraith that appears to our senses in the guise of a human entity that once, centuries ago, maybe, inhabited here, and is craving materialization.[2]

So how to apply a celebration of the golem as concept on concrete execution and tasks? In my own case, the first phase contained less thinking and more doing. In 2011, British artist Vicki Bennett invited Cotton Ferox (that is, Thomas Tibert and me) to make a piece of music for a program called "Radio Boredcast." As we had already been experimenting with magically charged texts within the confines of charged music, this turned out to be a very natural progression. The difference was that this became the first "Mega Golem Official Transmission." The text was written as the first investment in the "corpus"—in this case the Mega Golem's cock and balls, a suitable place to begin when creating something. I wrote the text, recorded it, and integrated it in the Cotton Ferox album (and film) *A Mega Golem Official Transmission:*

A Mega Golem Official Transmission
(Penis & Testicles)

The following is an official Mega Golem Broadcast Transmission of Cock and Balls presence and a declaration of moral independence in the digital ether. May the Mega Golem live long and prosper!

I'm envisioning time right now. Time is slow-moving, a soft staccato when we watch it, like the slow motion of the film and television segments we have grown up to love. We only see parts of the image flow we're supposed to in our mechanical sensory hegemony, and instead our minds try to patch up the fragments and make a new, more or less cohesive sequence; one that appears to be slow, regardless of whether the "measured" time from beginning to end is the same or not.

Measuring doesn't in any way indicate or display objective truth. Measuring is just a language in itself for those who speak measurian. Remember, for instance, that in the old days, sports used to be competition between individuals or teams of individuals. Today it is very much a self-righteous romance of measurement frenzy. Fractions of measured items and units are compared. Achievement is no longer a human trait of triumph but rather something that receives existence by the measurement and integration into the technology of statistics. Are we robots? Are we not? Well, *they* certainly are.

Let us therefore measure no more. The proof is not in the pudding any more than size matters. What matters is charge and discharge, passion, contrast, conflict, energy, ejaculation, emission, the strength of the moment in its own dissolving. There are no more supernovas or black holes in the universe, only an endless multicolored flow of energy that is a reflection of subjective truth. What's not to love about that? In fact, you can absolutely be that dissolved moment yourself. Please take some time—the slow kind—and think about it.

People seem happy to talk about the concept of the attention span but then they immediately forget why. If one more advertising campaign tells me that their product can simplify my life, I will have to use force in my decline of their offer. Nothing complicates more than new simplifications. Want simplicity? Well, begin by discarding all those simplifying tools. Want an attention span? Well, stop thinking about it. Want more time? Well, cease your agenda chopping. Want a slower time? Well, do less.

Time and time again, timeless time, philosophers have suggested remedies. They're all good in their own peculiar way. Do less doesn't mean that, literally or necessarily, but just do less in that contemporary manner that fragments your view into tiny pieces—all measurable of course—and instead do more in painting a bigger picture: your own picture. Reclaim your own mind and everything will be totally fine. You will be disillusioned and slightly bitter of course because you will realize that you have wasted exactly what you have now reclaimed: TIME. However, in the end nothing matters. But until then, some things do. Your own mind, for instance, and your own time.

So, okay, freedom is actually here now. It's a joy, a blessing, an existential goodie bag of options. Will is here too. Hi, Will! How are you? Doing well, I hope. Actually, I know you're doing well. I'm happy about it. We're meshed in the afternoon and around the clock of measured time. And outside the circles of that other time too, of course. "Love lifts us up where we belong."

So many options. So many potions. Diligence has paid off . . . doubt. Perseverance has paid off . . . persecution. I'm now in a position that is blessed, fully integrated in a Mega Golem's cock and balls. What a magnificent privilege. There will be others in the same position after me, I'm sure, but right now it does feel like a genuinely pioneering exploration of possibilities. My will be done! My will in the Mega Golem's cock and balls. Right-o, here we come!

The writing is read and the reading is right. Never have I been able to express myself any better than in that little sentence. It's like a prison sentence of an immeasurable freedom, a sui generis je ne sais quoi of a fait accompli that really sums me up. If I could tap and sell that, I'd be a gazillionaire. But of course it's neither tappable nor for sale, and I like that. And I'm still a gazillionaire of sorts.

Which brings us to pecuniary possibilities. They overflow. I am amazed. Have money? Here I am. Thank you very much. I'm polite and grateful and you have just been in contact with someone you probably needed to be in contact with. Simple as that. Every situation is a potential win-win situation and that's why the pecuniary flow passes through me but also leaves a staggering residue of affluence and a more-than-enoughish taint. Best to invest with zest at my own behest!

Now, what exactly is it that I do? Am I in the right position? Well, I look and see and then I recount in my own way. This has happened, take it or leave it. I used to think this was escapism or a psychological-emotional fulfilment, but it's not. It's about making a contribution to the unlimited collage, the Quantum Quilt, that is the overall human existence on this planet and in this omniverse. History-writing in four or even more dimensions. Yes, I write, I read, I cast an occasional spell, I aspire, I inspire, I take pictures, I make pictures like reflection surfaces, I'm the Mega Golem's cock and balls—a really privileged position to be in, I should add—and I enjoy it more than I dare to even admit (probably for superstitious reasons).

The activities and methods are fine and decidedly well modeled. A nice and functioning structure, on the whole and in the hole. The applications and implementations are being retuned and refocused, with great success. Diligence, perseverance, the ability to move slowly at a fast pace, self-discipline, honesty, and so forth. The usual suspects and ingredients are present.

The words affix themselves to the worlds. The worlds filter themselves through the words. The images are parts of the imaginations, the nations of images, all seeking each other out like grounded magnets, polarities, or cruising sybarites of the night. If we stop and look, we can see a pattern. Others can too, and are certainly willing to pay dearly for the privilege. Thank you very much. The pattern is a mind pattern and that pattern is mine. Imagination is the essence of the apprehension of truth that includes possibilities and makes every situation a potential win-win situation. Come to think about it, imagination is the only truth, with dreams a close-sniffing second: a brother in arms in the war against mechanical minds and the slaves of measurement and the slaves of their own uncut umbilical chords of empiricism. Fuck them until they fall asleep. Fuck them until they wake up. That's the task of the Mega Golem's cock and balls: to impregnate them with what they fear most: a reflection of themselves and everything they have denied themselves. Thank you very much.

But, please, let's not be dogmatic about it. Not polemical. Many of those who have trod in similar shoes before have failed because of the dogmatic, polemical aspects, the needs in themselves to compensate for their own essentially weak egos and neuroses. Much better to set a good example of self-preservation and success—and so much more enjoyable!—than to rant away mechanically until no one cares to listen.

The Mega Golem's cock and balls, ever ready, hard, and fertile. The orifices of your own ears have just been penetrated. It felt quite good, right? "Another time, another orifice"—that's my motto now. Free will. Free love. Responsibility to the responsible and good times all around!

"Adieu, adieu, parting is such sweet sorrow." But it's not a parting per se. It's only a parting of the veil. It's a new opening, a new orifice. It's just a temporary farewell, a little rest before new battles begin and new mind fields are ploughed. We can patch up the fragments now and slow things down, acting fast while appearing totally and irrevocably still. Still, moving. Still, life.

Not long after this film and spoken-word piece were finished, Cotton Ferox played in Warsaw, Poland. Knowing that this meant an excellent opportunity to go "full throttle" with the butterfly effect via sonic amplification, I decided to give birth to the actual Mega Golem being. Before this I had also extended invitations to artists I knew who are perceptive enough to understand the concept. I told them that if they wanted to, they could contribute a piece of art (any kind) to the Mega Golem. It could be a thought, a sentiment, or a piece of its multi-gender/hermaphroditic body. It could be visible, invisible, or indivisible. And they didn't even have to tell me about it either.

With the film being projected on stage, and with Thomas Tibert and Dr. Zaraza creating suggestive soundscapes behind me, I put on my red plastic devil mask and entered the birth pangs by reading the following poem:

MEGA GOLEM (BIRTH)

Mega Golem

Here you are

Mega Golem

Bright new star

Growing stronger

By the day

Growing longer

Here to stay

✳

Limbs of force
And fury too
No remorse
One love—or two

Art by art
Piece by piece
You are smart
And still at ease

Mega Golem
Do your thing
Mega Golem
In the swing

Of things to come
The Is to Be
Feared by some
Revered by me

So it is done!

And indeed it was! I felt elated, excited, aroused, and intensely satisfied. Now it was all beyond my control (such a wonderful feeling!). I had set the creature in motion, charged with my will, and I could now no longer perceive it with my own senses and sensibilities. The Mega Golem was born.

Some of my artist friends got in touch to learn more. A few let me know that they had indeed created something for the Mega Golem but didn't want to tell me exactly what. Which was perfectly fine. The project had already turned into a psychic, transdimensional exquisite corpse, and I could feel another contribution was forthcoming from myself. The following Cotton Ferox concert, in Stockholm in May 2014, offered another chance to go beyond the predictable spoken-word experience and instead ejaculate more Golemic seed. As there was now already (at least) a cock and balls, and life, there needed to be a continued breathing process. I put on the devil mask again and indulged in this:

ART SET FREE (BREATH)
Heed the letters
Heed the books
Heed the money
Feed the looks

A web of wonders
Near and far
A clearer picture
Of who we are

And can become
The Is to Be
And will become
The life in me

Open up the doors of markets
Open up the doors of art
Open up the doors of mind frames
This is just a humble start

The trap is dissolved
And art set free
For those involved
Both you and me

✳

In it goes and out it comes
Multiplying possibilities

Disinformation
Disinterest
Disintegration
Disposability
Dissemination
Distribution

Into the world we come
And it feels good

So mote it be!

Suddenly, the Mega Golem not only existed but started breathing regularly, still out there and still seeing all the worlds and dimensions. The next key ingredient of its system should then be the ability to not only live mechanically/predictably but also to appreciate and enhance life by creativity. Next stop: Libido! This was manifested in the spring of 2016, again in Warsaw, and again embraced by the sonorous safety of Cotton Ferox. No devil mask this time, but still in the same spirit:

UNFOLDING (FOR VANESSA) (LIBIDO)
Rising up from the dead
The sleeping, resting, waiting
Once again in material form
Temporarily in transit
Waiting to be delivered yet again
Welcome the possibilities
Anointed with witches' oil

A sublime transdimensional expression
Of Love
Welcome back
May it unfold in a life-enhancing way for us both
And for all involved
One step at a time
Will fix desire
It constrains the mobility of desire
There are no existential safety nets
When you don't exist
Bring it on
As always
Unfolding
Enhancing
Uniting
Creating
In the best possible way
Occupy both and all positions at once
Let's applaud being too privileged
For what has already been
Eternal thanks
For what is
Eternal thanks
For what's yet to come
Eternal thanks
Gratitude is sometimes not enough
But it is a currency that matters
In the big picture of life
Being blessed should not be taken for granted
Or lightly
Time breaks down barriers
As we break down the barriers of time

The wheel continues
A hypnagogic triumph
A hypnopompic truth
A ruse
Total allusion
A simile
An edge that pierces the crust
It eludes us
And instills within us all that we need
To know
To dare
To will
And to be silent

Shortly after this, an important contribution also appeared from the outside. The talented American occult philosopher and writer Kadmus sent in a poem for my annual occultural journal *The Fenris Wolf,* which gave the Mega Golem a healthy and steady heartbeat. This vitalized the creation as such, and I reinforced the poem by reading it out aloud on the launch evening for the publication in London in September of 2016.

A FRAGMENT OF HEART
(A CONTRIBUTION TO THE MEGA GOLEM
BY KADMUS)

Something stirs—
Where once rivers flowed,
Where the ghosts of trees rest
Unremembered.
Something wakens—
From concrete
Once mossy banks,
And blinks.

It cherishes—
How the crows used to gossip in the branches
Just so,
And the stones of the river winked
With hidden quartz.
It shelters—
The echoes of days without time
When walks went on forever
And we watched clouds play tag
With our backs bruised with grass stains.
Something smiles—
Where slim stalks will grow
And angry voices will rise in joy
To demand life for the earth
The voiceful wind
The wine-dark sea
The shivering wave
The silken sky
Once more.
Something remembers—
The songs we will strike
Like bonfires
In the fields at the end of history.
You can hear its voice calling us together
Hidden in the folds of the breeze
In the corners of the night
When no tread paces.
"Golem?" it asks,
"Call me Hope."

And this is where the Mega Golem now resides in time and space; alive, vital, sexual (to my knowledge, it currently has one penis and two vaginas—oh, lucky creature!), and willful. I have no idea where this will end, and actually suspect it never will. It definitely contains my charges, and possibly others' too, so it's preoccupied all right. Should you ever encounter the Mega Golem, be courteous. It may someday contain a part of you too, extended into the realms of magic, fantasy, and dreams—that is, the sphere of the ultimately real.

Hear and understand. The man who sought you out, and whom you call the Golem, signifies the awakening of the soul through the innermost life of the spirit. Each thing that earth contains is nothing more than an everlasting symbol clothed in dust. Learn how to think with your eyes. Think with your eyes, as you behold each and every shape. Nothing that takes shape unto itself but was once a spirit.[3]

15

Sexual-Dynamic Polarity as a Magical Formula

Aleister Crowley's Views on Gender and Transcendence

A lecture delivered at Odrörer Oasis OTO, Stockholm, Sweden, 2016.

WHEN TALKING ABOUT Aleister Crowley's views on sex and sexuality, you could absolutely say that he was ahead of his times. That was true of him as a person too, of course. On many levels, he was a synthesizing occult pioneer who initiated changes that would later become very important. Of course, he wasn't an isolated force during this general liberalization of the twentieth century. There were many individuals, things, and movements that opened up many radical developments.

Crowley's own environment and background, post-Victorian and bourgeois, wasn't only attacked by him but also, slightly earlier, by Oscar Wilde and his lover Alfred Douglas. This public scandal brought forth stronger reverberations than those Crowley would later create—much to his disdain and frustration of coursey. But the Wilde scandal was an interesting development at the time, as it broke not only sexual conventions but also other, more deeply rooted ones—specifically an audacious visibility in the public sphere. A certain sexual tolerance toward the cultural sphere has always existed, even in Great Britain.* If you cross more lines than the accepted quota, there will be conflict. But out of conflict something new and vital always arises.

The First World War was obviously a revolutionary force. The effects of four years of brutal war on European soil created an ever-faster swinging pendulum movement between a strongly defined and developed liberalism on the one hand, and a strong and elaborate totalitarianism in communism and National Socialism on the other. Women's liberation and their right to vote spread quickly in the democratic countries. Woman as a distinct member of society was now suddenly a force to be reckoned with.

For Crowley, who was born in 1875, this surely meant positive feelings on a philosophical level but perhaps slightly less so in the private sphere. Crowley's attitude toward women were about as complex as he himself was. When it came to abstracted individuals in a philosophical context every man and every woman was a star with the potential to find out his or her own voice and will. But when it came to his own relationships, things were, as it's nowadays said, complicated.

To a great degree, Crowley worked within a utilitarian mind frame, especially from the 1910s and onward. Regardless if we talk about longer relationships or brief rendezvous, Crowley literally wanted to use women as ejaculators of energies that can be directed and create new life in different forms, way, way beyond the conventions of petit bourgeois sexuality. For him, everything was ritual, regardless if the sexual partner in question was aware of it or not.

In Crowley's central text, *Liber AL* (*The Book of the Law*) there are many references to sexual mysteries and an all-encompassing new set

---

*For more on Aleister Crowley and Lord Alfred Douglas, please see Nina Antonia's "Bosie and the Beast," in Carl Abrahamsson, ed., *The Fenris Wolf*, no. 8 (Stockholm: Trapart Books, 2016).

of morals. At the time of the writing of this allegedly channeled text, Crowley wasn't initiated into sexual mysteries. The text confused and attracted him at the same time. But he did have an intuitive comprehension of how magic works, and he, according to himself at least, was a magical natural force that had appeared in order to change this planet's destiny in overturning ways. It wasn't until the 1910s, when he had been in touch with the German fraternal order Ordo Templi Orientis (OTO), that he and this group could create a synthesis of what both parties were interested in: sexual magic.

Liber AL is a cryptic text, difficult to interpret, and furthermore with an official decree that only Crowley in his position as scribe is really allowed to interpret it. The book consists of three chapters, each one clothed in Egyptian terminology. The first chapter, dedicated to the goddess Nuit, describes infinite cosmic potential. In this potential there is pleasure, beauty, and attractional force, but it's not tangible or perceivable before you have a direction, a goal. This constitutes chapter two, dedicated to Hadit (not to be confused with the Hadith, the prophet Muhammad's moral codex). When Nuit and Hadit meet in union there is Ra-Hoor-Khuit, which traditionally is an aspect of the main solar deity Ra. In this union exists an aggressive energy with the power both to create and destroy. This trio is what constitutes magical potential in Crowley's cosmology.

In the text there is implicitly a formulation or formula that replaces previous magical formulas stemming from Judeo-Christian sources. This is called $0 = 2$ or, by simple mathematical logic, $2 = 0$. Crowley explained it like this: "Every act of 'love under will' has the dual result 1) the creation of a child combining the qualities of its parents, 2) the withdrawal by ecstasy into Nothingness."[1] Just as division of a unity leads to two parts, these two parts can create not only a new unity but also a dissolution in and through the unity in question. Where classic magical formula making up until then had been built on a literally familiar order of succession (Yod, He, Vau, He, Father, Mother, Son,

Daughter, new life, etc.), we can now see a considerably more Asian attitude in Crowley's mind.

Most of us are aware, both on instinctive and personal levels, that sex is the most potent form of energy a human being can experience. There is not only the possibility to create new human life but also, at the moment of orgasm, to be an active part of a transcendental experience without comparison. Sex has always been present in magical and religious contexts as a very fundamental part. Either as liberating or enslaving, depending on the society, culture, or reigning power structure in question.

There were other interesting things going on at this time than Crowley's awakenings and fascinating Oscar Wilde scandals. Within physics the terms *fusion* and *fission* were clarified and codified. That is, the setting free of energy in the interaction of atoms, either through merging or splitting. Put simply: the stronger the attraction is between or within atoms, the stronger the energy set free in the meeting. The Danish scientist Niels Bohr's work with establishing what was to be called quantum mechanical principles in the energy flows of atoms led to his Nobel Prize in 1922. The German scientist Karl Heisenberg was another giant who received the Nobel Prize in 1932 for the development of quantum mechanics. The relationship between quantum mechanics and magic as a proto-science is so strong that you can almost say that it doesn't appear to be random that both magic and radical physics developed so quickly and in such a parallel way during the early twentieth century.

We can talk about it on a human existential level, on a microlevel in atomic perspectives, and on a larger, cosmic level. The sun and the stars simply exist and generate so much energy that it makes our lives possible and facilitates my standing here talking and you listening. Crowley was well aware of these fundamental scientific basics and often referred to a scientific, empirical method in his works. He also called his system "solar-phallic." The sun is in many ways the highest divine principle and it's fueled by fusion energy. The highest tangible level or mirroring within the human being of this solar-phallic power is sex, and its main representative, according to Crowley, the male sexual organ.

However, this is not synonymous with phallic worship, which has been a consistent part of human religious history. The interesting thing from a magico-anthropological perspective is that phallic worship seemed to cease as humans left a holistic attitude within fertility cults and natural religion, not seldom containing hermaphroditic ideals, in favor of a dualism in which man is regarded as active and woman passive—decidedly an Abrahamic, monotheistic metaphor for power structures rather than sexual dynamics per se.

Crowley formulated that the emerging aeon was in need of new magical systems: "The true magick of Horus requires the passionate union of opposites."[2] This also goes well beyond the merely sexual metaphor. *Passionate* doesn't necessarily mean loving or even benevolent. Big political cataclysms during which opponents clash often lead to constructive third-side solutions, either through compromise or unexpected quantum leaps. And they can certainly be passionate. It is within the unique moment where diametrical forces clash that energy is set free. If you have insight, understanding, and respect it's absolutely possible to direct this energy toward new goals.

Crowley felt overwhelmed by *Liber AL,* meaning "honor and duty bound," and obligated to interpret the mysteries of the text. His entire magical work and authorship would soon focus on the creation of Thelema, a philosophy stemming from *Liber AL.* And that's basically how it continued all the way up until his death in 1947.

The OTO contained a more concrete structure, which attracted Crowley. The sources of the group's teachings and mysteries have later been criticized for being not only mystical but also mythical. According to this possible myth the order received both textual sources and oral teachings and initiations from Asia via the Middle East. These thoughts or streams were in no way new but rather signs of a budding cosmopolitan knowledge and interest at the end of the nineteenth century, via an opening up of Asia Minor as well as Major. Perhaps this was in many ways a romanticized current, but that in no way makes the phenomenon less substantial or valid. The OTO quickly became an attractive fraternity among Freemasons who were lured in by the sexual mysteries themselves but also by the pretty relevant fact that here, even women were allowed initiation. Eventually, a synthesis of both parts was created: the German organization with a distinctly Freemasonic, albeit open-minded, structure and the chaotic Great Beast Crowley's Thelema philosophy and its magical excellence.

The books *Hymns to the Goddess* and *Tantra of the Great Liberation,* written by Arthur Avalon (John Woodroffe) and both published in 1913, brought in Hindu magical aspects to Western minds. The slightly later *Shakti & Shakta* (1918) and *The Serpent Power* (1919) carried on Avalon's popularization of terms or notions like tantrism and kundalini yoga. Another parallel strain was the German Richard Wilhelm, whose translations from the Chinese were relevant in this context. His *Secret of the Golden Flower* was published in English in 1931, with an introduction by Carl Jung, and was an important insight into sexual aspects of Taoism. Taoism had become increasingly important for Crowley after a specifically Taoist epiphany or illumination in America in 1918: "Whoever seeks eternal life must search for the place whence human nature and life originally sprang."[3]

Crowley's integration of the *I-Ching,* the *Book of Changes,* maybe didn't have a distinctly sexual importance, but it's indicative of an openness to cultures whose work with sexual magical techniques had up until this time been fairly unknown, or "mythical." It was as if the time was now ripe for universal secrets concerning proto-generative energies to emerge from the depths and be reformulated by Westerners, either through translations (Wilhelm) or synthesis (Crowley, OTO). This didn't necessarily mean instant explanations of everything for an unenlightened mass of people but definitely an availability of material and thereby an opportunity for proper studies.

Crowley's Gnostic Mass, written in 1913, became central in his life and system within the OTO, and still is. The idea was that this ceremony would be as central within the OTO and Thelema as the Catholic Mass within the Roman Catholic Church. For Crowley and his followers, the ceremonial performance of an intimate act, loaded with sexual symbolism and secrets from many different esoteric traditions, became a celebration of the proto-generative force in a sublime and aestheticized form. Crowley, who was scientifically inclined, was also concerned that he "would neither make nor imply any statement about nature which would not be endorsed by the most materialistic man of science."[4]

One section in the Gnostic Mass is the honoring of what Crowley called the gnostic saints. This is a long and thorough list of mythical and actual persons who directly or, most often, indirectly, helped out with the development of Thelema. Remarkably, the list consists only of men, which has led to many interesting debates and discussions within the Thelemic environment. Should one here simply regard Crowley as a child of his times, or was he actually just a male chauvinist pig? Or could it possibly be, as has been claimed, that the potential of women lies far beyond and above these worldly men's destinies and manifestations? In an aggressively gender-baiting intellectual climate like ours it's not surprising that this issue stirs up emotions. But at the same time it's easy to see who is actually placed on the altar in the ceremony and who is worshiped not only as a concrete life giver but also as a metaphorical catalyst for all creation. Perhaps this is best expressed in the famous words of wisdom: "If you want something said, ask a man. If you want something done, ask a woman." (Margaret Thatcher)

The list of possible female gnostic saints could of course be quite long. Perhaps it wouldn't actually contain Margaret Thatcher, but most definitely the woman who uttered "Is that a gun in your pocket or are you just glad to see me?" (Mae West)

Sexual insights, techniques, and rituals were incorporated in the existing hierarchical degree system of the OTO. Crowley explored all of this intensely after he had received a carte blanche to study the degrees, and also to develop them. In this fervent work as not only a magician but now also a sex magician, Crowley naturally needed someone to work with. Perhaps his German Freemason brothers weren't the most attractive candidates in this sexual context. The need for willing women became clear and urgent, women who were either attracted by the "Great Beast" in Crowley, by his reputation, or who simply didn't have a clue what was going on on the astral planes during these cosmic sexual congresses.

For Crowley, who in his bisexuality was a submissive homosexual, it was natural to experiment with homosexual energies within ritual contexts. And here we come to an interesting magical crossroads in this reasoning and story: How do homosexual activities work in a so-called sexual-dynamic polarity? The answer is, in exactly the same way as during heterosexual congress. There may be an initial sexual confusion (for outsiders) on the energy level, meaning there are two men or two women having sex. But what it all still boils down to is that two distinctly different energies have to meet to maximize the discharge with its inherent transcendental potential. The homosexual meeting can also in itself be transcendentally liberating if you look at it in the context of, for instance, a prejudiced or condemning surrounding. In that conflict, there is also a diametrical challenge that can be overcome and used creatively.

Crowley formulated this magical principle in the term *Babalon*. Going back to the romantic notion of the Whore of Babylon in the so-called Revelation of the Christian Bible, he created an attractive rebellious principle that appealed both to his own fantasies and to women with a need to free themselves from patriarchal stereotypes. But the term contains much more than his own poetic definitions of personal preferences. The Babalon concept is a central part of the sex-magical teachings and techniques within the OTO and also within other organizations. The formula I mentioned earlier, $2 = 0$, is an important key to this. Two parts, or rather two poles, make possible a temporary setting free of energy in transcendence, which can be used in ritual contexts. But it's far too easy to get stuck in stereotypes or stagnant concepts in which rebellious archetypes quickly become reactionary.*

One clear example of an intellectually based sadomasochism that was typical of Crowley exists in Leah Hirsig's oath to Crowley during the early 1920s at Cefalu, where Crowley had created an Abbey of Thelema, a monastery of sorts where Thelemites could develop themselves. Hirsig was one of Crowley's main "scarlet women" or magical partners. They worked ritually together, imbued by the Babalon concept and inspired by the force set free in their sexual escapades.

> *I dedicate myself wholly without stint to the Great Work.*
> *I will raise myself in pride:*
> *I will follow Ra-Hoor-Khuit in His way:*
> *I will work the way of wickedness:*
> *I will kill my heart:*
> *I will be loud and adulterous:*
> *I will be covered with jewels and rich garments:*
> *I will be shameless before all men:*
> *I, for token thereof, will freely prostitute my body to the*
>   *lusts of each and every Living Creature that shall*
>   *desire it:*
> *I claim the title Mystery of Mysteries, BABALON the*
>   *Great and the Number 156, and the Robe of the*
>   *Woman of Whoredoms and the Cup of*
>   *Abominations:*
>
> *Witness mine Hand. Alostrael*[5]

---

*For more on my interpretation of the Babalon concept and formula, please see "Babalon" in *The Fenris Wolf,* no. 6 (Stockholm: Edda Publishing, 2013).

The question now becomes: How much of this is (*a*) a genuinely intuitive yet willed magical formulation; (*b*) Crowley's sexual fantasies; or (*c*) Hirsig's own sexual fantasies?

Crowley's life is undoubtedly a story of complex relationships to both men and women, sexually as well as emotionally. It's easy to criticize too harshly and claim that he used people financially and sexually. But at the same time we mustn't forget that his work as a philosopher and author shows a considerably more altruistic, albeit distinctly post-Nietzschean, side that encourages all men and women's undeniable potential and right to individual liberty. Crowley is certainly not alone in creating a great pathos of freedom and benevolence on a theoretical plane while he himself at times had obvious problems with the implementation on practical levels.

Aleister Crowley was a child of his time, whose emotional cluster was built on a hatred of his upbringing in general and of his mother in particular. His integration of a feminine sexual role in the homosexual contacts and a rough, dominant masculine role in the heterosexual contacts seems to indicate some kind of dissolution of core identity. As these behaviors were integrated *before* his magical awakenings and initiations, we must suppose that these later integrations of the roles as distinct magical energies to a great extent were *ex post facto* constructions—albeit very creative and usable ones.

Crowley was a genuine researcher who unfortunately quite often drifted into either benevolent hedonism or malevolent addiction. It's perfectly legitimate to ask oneself whether his own experienced shortcomings were necessities he turned into virtues. I'm thinking both of his flamboyant bisexuality and his abuse of drugs. Maybe the related stigma at the time was easier to deal with on a personal, emotional level if he created an intricate raison d'être that turned both these areas into constructive building blocks in a personal, magical universe? I have a hard time believing that the specifically transcendental aspects of both these traits were used or integrated by him fully *all* the time and totally consciously.

This entire line of reasoning also leads to a metaphysical speculation about the need for development. If the distinctly magical—that is, the potentially supra-creative—lies in the discharge between diametrical poles, then routine-based "normal" polarities should eventually become dissolved or weakened. A concrete example of this could be a human relationship that is diminishing after the sexual element within the relationship has weakened.

Crowley's Babalon concept is not built upon the assumption that all women must be loose or emancipated on terms dictated by certain men. It is rather based on rebellion within context. Everything that moves on in routine is eventually weakened and loses its right to exist. The stereotypical image of the Babalon archetype we can see in the Lust card in the Thoth Tarot deck and within the global Thelemic community, with a naked woman straddling a lion, is far from as controversial today as it was a century or even longer ago. The sexual neuroses and bad trips of the biblical authors for a long time created enormous possibilities for magical work inside the sexual-dynamic polarity and provocation. There and then, the "scarlet woman" was a potent symbol of emancipation. The more rigid and strict the conventions, the easier to rebel and thereby set free energy for magical purposes.

This leads on to the question: What or who is Babalon today? I don't think it's feminists with bright neon hair colors and hundreds of university degrees in gender studies. Nor is it politically correct Net-based hipsters and social media *rabulists* and fabulists who usually, paradoxically, are completely intolerant toward anyone with a divergent point of view. A Babalon today, as always, is simply the person who dares defy the current norms or hegemonies, regardless if they exist on private, sexual planes or general, existential ones. The opposition you encounter within a restrictive sphere is the actual tool that can liberate enormous energies in favor of your own creativity and success.

This also leads on to an important aspect that must never be forgotten. We all exist within *individual* contexts. Crowley's Thelema philosophy is about individualism, about an enlightened egoism in which you assume responsibility for your own life and your own choices. All collective processes eventually lead to philosophical and moral stagnation. Unfortunately, it's in the unenlightened human nature to proceed and advance at the cost of others. What could be easier than to hide behind a group or a collective ideal and become a spokesperson for other basically free individuals without asking for permission first? Regardless if you're a man or a woman or something else, and no matter what you fight for, I think it's important to remember that you are only you. That personal sphere in itself is an enormous responsibility.

16

The Economy of Magic

There's No Free Lunch or Free Magical Success

*Originally a lecture delivered at Nekropolis Bogcafé
in Copenhagen, Denmark, 2015.*

IN SEVERAL SEQUENCES of the TV series *Carnivale* we can see the protagonist Ben Hawkins heal wounds and even bring people back from the dead. It looks impressive, but the process takes a toll on the young, almost unwilling magician. It's because he knows there's a price to pay. Around him, the vital energy needed for the operation at hand is always sucked from someone or something else. Human beings, fields of crops, and birds perish when he transfers that energy into the dead and the injured.

The equation is obvious and brings us to the quintessential magical dilemma: You get, you give. You give, you get. It's there in that classic Faustian deal and it is there as a basis for all kinds of sacrificial rituals, from the smallest of cults to the greatest of the world's religions. And we can look at it from the smallest level of personal need or greed and up to global or even cosmic interrelationships.

Although this is essentially a well-known axiom or equation all through various myths and teachings, I still notice that many young occultists within a Western sphere school themselves, or are schooled, in a kind of smash-and-grab mentality. This undoubtedly ties in with a general Occidental mind frame in which it's apparently possible to just get and get and get. But we all know that somewhere in a third world country or at sea rests the toxic debris and waste of that attitude, which in turn is or will be eventually impossible to escape for *anyone* residing on this planet.

For the Occidental occultist mind, quite often with no ties to larger moral or religious clusters, it seems possible to command spirits, demons, or other kinds of forces merely because it's his or her will. The Occidental presents endless series of demands, in which the mere opening of the door and greeting should bring success and manifestation. It should be made clear, though, that this is not how things work. Not on the smallest of small levels, and not on the grandest of grand scales.

Whether looking at outer or inner process, there's a balance that needs to be set. The equation of supply, demand, and cost is all-pervading. Everything requires something to be able to produce the force or item that's desired. The complicated web of outer productivity seems banal but serves as a good example: someone spends time and energy to make something that is then sold to a buyer, who pays for it with the magical energy of money, that in turn has been procured somehow in other generative circles.

This is the most basic example of a relationship that permeates everything around us and in us. It's almost as if it's a general fundament, a prerequisite of civilized life. The mere demanding without willingness to give anything back is then a suggestion of massive potential or actual failure.

If we begin on the grand scale, which is no less magical than the incense-clouded personal temples, we can see that in the major myths, there has always been some kind of existential sacrifice involved. Two main examples: the human being Jesus became a christic force by sacrificing his life with determination and free will. This created a phantasmagoric residue, a psychopomp that was then integrated by the

Christian power structure as myth. The focus was on the deed itself and its implications. "Jesus died for *your* sins," implying a transference of sacrificial magical energy beyond the realm of the personal human being Jesus. This, handled by a clever organization, can apparently work wonders too.

A second example: the Buddha reached enlightenment by realizing the necessity of balance, where neither death-related ascetic behavior nor sensual debauchery was favored. In samsara, the world of the senses, it was necessary to renounce these extremes and also important to embrace the concept of karma, meaning in this context *not* "you will get good things and possible release from samsara if you do good things" but rather "if you do good things, you will get good things and possible release from samsara." Although both positions are logically the same, morally they're not.

Long before this, a similar concept was in use in Egyptian mythology. The heart of a deceased person would be weighed on scales against the feather of Maat, the goddess of truth, by Anubis, god of the afterlife. If it was pure, everything was fine, and the deceased could move on to afterlife. If not, the heart would be devoured by the demon Ammit. The heart's purity was defined by the moral standards of the day, and the tool used was a central one in economy and trade: the scales.

As a cosmic principle, karma could be said to exist—meaning the books need to be balanced or there will be extra taxation or perhaps even investigation of fraud or tax evasion. Water always finds its own level. On a personal level, though, karma is mainly a cultural concept that has seeped into the West from the East. The term itself thus becomes entangled with both religious and moral issues, which creates an unnecessarily complex overview. In its place in this context I would therefore like to substitute the term *magicoin*. Sure, *magical currency* could be another suitable term, but this easily becomes semantically entangled with other kinds of concepts within the magical sphere (the 93 current, the Setian current, etc.).

In our Western sphere, self and will rule supreme. And this is as it should be: without self-knowledge and will, we get nowhere; or perhaps, at most, we get shuffled around by others who are more eloquent in defining us and who thereby can use us for their own ends. But if self and will are there, firmly rooted within the individual, we have a good, solid foundation to learn about how magic (and life) works. If we stay on the level of "I want" without further understanding of genuine *magicoin* principles, there will be debt. If we work with agents like spirits or other nontangible, inner forces, we can only go so far with a steady flow of demands—just as with credit cards.

It's almost easier to understand the *magicoin* principle when looking at it outside the sphere of magic. Money is one very clear sphere; human relationships another. If we take something and don't pay, that's called stealing. If we use someone else indefinitely for our own ends, that turns into abuse and, very likely, confrontation. That's why we don't do those things if we see the big picture and understand our own position within it.

Why is the dilemma even there? That is, why is it that magicians in the Western sphere so seldom understand these basic principles? I think the problem is twofold. One is that magical practice is usually compartmentalized in time and space and seen as an activity separate from the overall flow of life. This is a big error. If magical practice is fully integrated in one's life, for instance, by applying one's own terms and interpretations rather than rehashing traditional, dogmatic, symbolic, and arcane ones (and thereby also increasing the potential for a better understanding of the concepts), there won't even be any dilemma left. Hermes Trismegistus's dictum of "As above, so below" will rule on all levels, both outer and inner.

The second aspect is that I perceive that many young people begin with magical practice before they're fully individuated. That is, before they fully understand their own relationship to everyone and everything else. Magic is mistakenly regarded simply as something you *do* at certain times and spaces, not something you *are* 24/7 and wherever you go or stay. Magic is mistakenly regarded simply as something you do to achieve your own ends in fairly nonrational ways, *not* something that ties you together holistically with the universe.

It's a bit like cramming in school. Students can mechanically or automatically repeat what's been taught in class and thereby give a semblance of knowing. Which can, in bad schools, actually produce good grades. But these are grades that are misleading as indications of real understanding. Any challenging or unexpected question to the student will quickly reveal that it's just a matter of regurgitation or repetition.

By being, we carry potential. By doing, we achieve. But by achieving, are we always successful? What we do affects us on the inner planes, and also the totality outside us. If we disregard any overall karmic concepts as being strictly moral ones, and instead just look to the economy of the processes, it is my experience that if there's a conscious and willed balance in the magicoin books, there *will* be success.

It's always healthier to *generate* funds than it is to deal with credit—this is something most of us recognize from everyday finances—and how we generate is by offering first and asking later. It's interesting to see how the word *offer* even ties in etymologically to this. *To sacrifice* means "to make holy." The German word for "victim" and for "sacrifice" itself is *Opfer* (in Swedish "to sacrifice" is *att offra;* cf. "make an offer"). The word *victim* is originally Latin, and means exactly the same as in English. Its roots can be traced to a "sacrificed animal." Another synonym for something sacrificed is *hostia,* as for instance in the "host" of the Christian communion, and as in the English *hostage,* something or someone being offered in return for something or someone else.

Is magical success equal to the concept of profit? That is, if we generate more than what we spend, is that a sign of specific magical success? The answer is no. Profit and surplus are in our minds predominantly an economic, cultural concept within a tradition, not an existential given. Of course, one could argue that financial profit and its residues are necessary as status indicators and thereby of natural stratifying processes. However, the magical process is always an individual one. It can never be collective. Magical success equals the balancing of the individual magicoin books. One exception would be when advanced magicians actually contain more magicoin energy than they need for their own individual purposes. This can then be shared with others. If someone not advanced enough tries to do the same thing, there will be depletion and chaos within his or her own magicoin system.

Goethe's *Faust* is an often-referenced work of art in this regard, as is Marlowe's earlier play and a hundred different variants of the theme. Making a pact or a deal with the so-called devil is merely succumbing to a credit-based slavery situation. The same goes for working within traditional esoteric systems where so-called external forces are called forth to presence. If and when the magician declares his or her will to the force in question, but forgets to explain the possible dividends or even to add a *please* or *thank you* after the declaration, the odds are likely that the outcome will be more expensive than could ever be imagined.

What this means in real life is of course not that some occult force pops up at night and demands to be paid back in full or that some fantastic devil tries to drag your soul to some monotheistic vision of hell. But what it could mean is that you, after a successful ritual, find that its manifested goal may contain problematic aspects too, previously not considered. Had the preritual overview been crystal clear (the equivalent of an economic budget that balances out), problems could have been foreseen and possibly dealt with even before the ritual. An example: you perform a ritual to secure one more or less constant sexual partner. This manifests in a perfectly sexually compatible woman and she is very nice indeed. But she's also a human being with emotions and a will of her own that might not be compatible when she's making demands for a deeper relationship than one merely carnal. Or that as a result of the volatile and intense lust she's able to provoke, all according to your fantasies, you make her pregnant.

Another example could be an even more youthful or naive one: A young magician wants a gadget that he can't afford right now and performs a ritual for the situation. The train of events leads to that a good friend of his, equally poor, actually steals two gadgets and gives him one. This could be seen as a beautiful and successful operation from the magician's perspective. However, the friend was caught on CCTV and is later charged with the crime. The attraction of that gadget very soon loses its potency.

It would be much better to generate the energy needed oneself and then send it off on adventures of manifestation. If well directed, it not only becomes an appropriate legitimate expense but also potentially an investment—that is, an expense that furthers the cause, broadens the base, facilitates creative expansion. In the example of the fencing young magician, things could have been changed for the better with mere expression of intent. If he had integrated the expression of desire in a larger context of self-development for instance, in which the gadget could play a tangible, creative part, the result could have manifested in a different way, and his using the gadget lead to an improved skill rather than a bad conscience.

As in our normal economy, there is also a meta-level in the magic business. We normally talk about a stock market that trades in worth, loss, and potential in existing companies. Translated into our own sphere of hocus-pocus this would correspond to the lucrative area of magical books. They carry potential for change on their pages, and attract by symbolism, poetry, promises of power, and so forth. They deal with magic and they deal in magic. Thereby the entire meta-sphere of magical literature and its writers becomes the stock market of occultism, a realm of speculation in worth and potential. If more people invest in one writer rather than another, even though these writers may be writing about the same kinds of magical phenomena, then his or her value increases and even more investors show up. This could also strengthen related power structures such as magical groups or orders behind the writer in question, which could then be seen as an actual or an advisory board for the writer/corporation in question.

When the Catholic conquistadores entered Central America and were shocked by the human sacrifices performed by the Aztecs, they apparently forgot about the essence of their own religion. The Aztecs tried their best to appease their main sun god and other minor gods and goddesses by ritually killing human beings. In their own minds they succeeded, because the sun did come back. Every day, in fact. And crops and harvests were for the most part plentiful in that fertile region. So in a way they existed within a brutal and blood-soaked logic of success. The very same logic was then applied by the conquistadores, who slaughtered and eradicated the Aztecs and their behavior for their own profit and for Catholicism. They also succeeded: the Aztecs were killed off and Catholic success and affluence followed, which meant the remaining converts could now instead partake of communion consisting of blood and flesh from the invaders' own sacrificial proxy, Jesus Christ.

Today, human sacrifice is not condoned, if we exclude fundamentalist Muslim terrorists and some retrograde tribes in remote jungles. The challenge today, if we stick to our young hubristic Western magicians, is rather to deal with a culture of fragmentation and oversaturation. If we already have everything and still want more, wouldn't the most rewarding sacrifice have more to do with behaviors and attitudes rather than with tangible objects or life-forms? Cleaning up internally first, so to speak? Getting rid of destructive behavioral patterns and shortsightedness? Sacrificing external pollution and internal malnutrition?

An interesting yet considerably more speculative area of magico-economic research could be whether the magical currency (NB, *not* "current") is exchangeable or universal. Would it, for instance, be meaningful to use Scandinavian heathen magic in central Africa, or would one need to somehow exchange the terminology and the forces used for a successful operation? Would American Indian magic work well in Tibet? Aboriginal magic in the Vatican? Or vice versa?

Interesting things are also going on within the highly abstracted sphere of high finance in regard to Mother Nature's capital, which in many ways is permeated by powerful sources of magic. Where an old-fashioned economic thinking simply got what it wanted from the planet without returning anything at all (a very black form of magic) and thereby facilitated incredible fortunes out of many magical and sensitive ecosystems, today the phenomenon of "mitigation banking" is a new growth market in the undertow of ecological consciousness (or simply a bad conscience). It works like this: A bank buys a huge piece of land that needs protection for the sake of, for instance, biodiversity. Rapacious corporations can then buy or lease a small segment to exploit, quite expensively, and part of the bank's revenue then goes to actual further bioprotection. It's a very strange setup, almost illogical, but it's now making huge profits for all concerned. And yes, to perhaps a greater extent than in recent decades, wildlife can now be better protected. But it does have a strange, almost eerie aftertaste. It's like a bank suddenly owning a previously raped woman, and now, in the name of her overall protection, sells long-term leases on her body to her previous rapists. Translated into a magical setup, it's like a mitigation made by a wise magician for an assortment of unwise magicians, who all want to have results immediately but cannot see the big picture or the role they play. They can use the force but only when sanctioned by some other magician who is thereby getting morally and inexorably entangled in whatever it is that's going on. A healthy setup? I think not.

On a stricter and more concretely generative level, we can always return to the main mysteries of magic—the sexual ones—for both metaphor and concrete food for thought. The theory is usually divided into psychosexual and physical-residual parts. Isolationists say the creative force lies in one but not the other, and other, more holistically inclined theorists say it's a mix of both. That is, that the magical force lies in the ecstatic moment itself, which can be charged and directed, or that the dissemination and direction of the ultra-proto-generative force in the physical sperm and egg is what matters.

It's interesting to note, though, that the physical sacrifice of sperm in ejaculation carries almost unlimited potential when it comes to generating new human life. Even if there is conception, that was made possible by the parallel sacrifice of a billion sperm-buddies. Male generative sacrifice is usually associated with intense pleasure. Female generative sacrifice is usually associated with intense displeasure. The sacrifice of an unfertilized egg in menstruation is not such an apparent joyous occasion, but it does facilitate the placement of new egg, ready and willing should a vital sperm drop by. Considering the potential these generative sacrifices contain, both as states of mind *and* body, both as ecstasies *and* physical residue, it's no wonder that they constitute prime magical currency. With this very basic insight in mind, it should be easy to see that a credit-based magical economy might not be the best place to begin your own magical career.

Essentially, it's very simple: plus and minus need to add up to zero, in magical operations and in life in general. That's quite enough. If we can learn to change from looking at *sacrifice* as a painful noun to looking at it as a pleasurable, constructive verb, we have come a long way.

17

The Magic of Dreams
Made Real

*Originally a lecture delivered at Aleph
in Skopje, Macedonia, 2014.*

IN OUR CONTEMPORARY CULTURE the dream sphere has been moved to a mystical and stigmatized corner. It's a sphere that we usually try to understand by simplified interpretation models and a superstitious rationality. One of those interpretation models is the hierarchic one. This doesn't merely come from Freud but from a much larger background and perspective. But if we stick with Freud's powerful legacy, we recognize the hierarchic structure: id, ego, superego, and so on. It's a model we've grown accustomed to, as we have with his dream theories, claiming that the subconscious lies beneath and occasionally stirs up things when we let our guards down, reminding us of wishes, desires, fears, and frustrations. One central element in this model is that the rational mind runs the show when we're awake.

But there's no escaping the fact that we sleep and thereby dream approximately one-third of our lives. That's a lot of time and a lot of energy spent on something that is generally regarded as passive and irrational. Strangely enough, this perspective seems predominant even within contemporary psychology—at least that's how it's being taught today at American universities. The focus here seems to be on clinical experiments, neurology, and neurochemistry. But that in itself contains the same fundamental dilemma as most of the natural sciences: the beauty of a flower cannot be understood by dissecting it over and over again and trying to find out which chemicals are involved.

Quoting the American psychology professor Roger Knudson, a critical voice: "American psychology majors learn that dreams are meaningless by-products of brain processes. This is taught by every textbook in introductory psychology used in our department over the past decade." Also: "Imagination is mainly a source of error in memory and therefore is not to be trusted."[1] Freud was a child of his times, and the authoritarian, hierarchic thinking was in his case based both on his own religious environment and the overall European culture of postindustrial rationalism. Of course, we can absolutely *not* say that Freud regarded dreams and their importance as insignificant. Quite the contrary. But he worked within a context where focus on order was essential. Otherwise, in the dualistic logic that reigned supreme, everything would turn into chaos and inner disturbances.

Parallel to Freud's work were other manifestations of progress within the natural sciences, some of which unleashed enormous energies, for good and bad. The atomic structure theory, with its protonic center and a varying amount of electrons in orbit, quickly generated metaphysical speculations concerning the similarities with the structure of the universe. The atomic model of interpretation of both an inner and outer world is in many ways more usable in most contexts. It seems as though the hierarchic one fits best in processes that are rigid in their focus on pecking order, that is, ascribing to something a relative value: the higher is worth more than the lower, and so on. That kind of value-related thinking doesn't really exist within the atomic model.

We're going to stick with the atomic here. If we begin on an overall human level and look at the protonic center, we might as well call that core the individual. Around the individual many important phenomena and energies spin in orbit and make up the individual's makeup, so to speak. One model could be time and function based: one-third consists of awake work, one-third of awake social life, and one-third of sleeping/dreaming. Another model could be the sleeping third, where the proton could still be seen as the individual and the electrons could be physical repose and different types of dreaming. Or even different specific dreams.

On a very basic level our existence is all about reproduction and pushing life onward within our own species. That could seem to be a quite dull and hopeless existence but the human being, as an advanced cultural phenomenon, can at least find comfort in personal qualities and traits as the foundation for individual harmony. We apparently nurture a need to feel meaning and purpose. And to a varying degree we also do have the possibility to achieve these in our lives.

What it all boils down to is survival. Our bodies need to survive for as long as possible, and our greater collectives too. And on the individual level it's equally important to feel substance and meaning to be able to survive emotionally.

With this in mind we can see how our two waking thirds are very adapted for survival. We deal with what needs to be done to provide nutrition, protection, and shelter, and we work together with greater or smaller collectives to create a solid base for survival.

Is it then unlikely that the sleeping and thereby dreaming third is also a part of this survival strategy? Of course not. In fact, this could be the most important third of them all.

Sleeping isn't merely a passive resting but allows for the physical organism to very actively repair itself after two-thirds of stressing, wearing, and tearing. And consciousness enters another and higher gear to facilitate for other forms of information exchanges and reasonings. This too is to facilitate the survival of the totality.

To consider dreaming as a merely neurological process of order after a day of exposure to fragmented impressions, possibly with some unfulfilled desires thrown into the dream stew, is a presumptuous and demeaning example of how our contemporary times denigrate individuals to utilitarian units inside a soulless collective.

However, we're not supposed to be dealing with zeitgeist criticism here. Not this time. So let's stay with the function of the dreaming. Just as we communicate with our near and dear ones, work colleagues, and others during the two waking thirds in specific and conventional ways, the very same things happen with other consciousnesses during dreaming. The function of the dreaming is communicating, reflecting, reasoning, and instructing.

The questions then arise: With whom? From whom? About what? The most common piece of criticism is that it's not possible to prove that the dream sphere is mainly instructive since empirical experiments haven't been created to validate the theories. Well, not yet anyway. On a realistic level, though, this critical perspective fails. Only a fraction of all users can in detail explain how the Internet works on an empirically acceptable level, but that certainly doesn't stop them from communicating with each other, not seldom with entirely strange or new acquaintances and in new ways, and not seldom with the conscious purpose to learn about something or someone, and while at it also learn more about oneself.

A fragmented dream recall is a big problem and it's predominantly a cultural one. In many cultures where dreams and dreaming in general are given a higher status, the recall is more detailed, denser, and longer. In our own sphere, we often wake up via aggressive cell phone signals and thereby lose out on a soft hypnopompic agitation. If one is aware of it, there's always the possibility to adapt one's waking up a bit. Softer alarm signals and clocks with pulsating light are a few examples. It's interesting to see how this has recently been implemented in transcontinental flights. Instead of brutally just switching the lights on in the cabin when it's time to prepare for landing, soft, pulsating, and psychedelic multicolored lights now bring the passengers "back" to a waking state. Incidentally (?) these airplane models are called "dream liners."

It's totally possible to approach one's own dreaming. The first step is simply to value the meaning of the dreaming in itself, not merely as an intellectual or mental perspective or approach but by integrating the process as being absolutely essential, that is, necessary for living. A dream diary or notebook by your bedside is good, or perhaps having a little tape recorder that you can just talk straight into. That is interesting for the sake of dream substance but also because you consciously leave the hypnopompic comfort to be able to "report" to yourself. It's a self-disciplined method that leads to increased recall on all levels: frequency, intensity, length, and so on.

Another central aspect of valuing is the interpretation process. We live in the midst of a post-Freudian and sometimes post-Jungian world of interpretation, and many of their theories and models are totally dominant today. Many of them are still useful, but the most important thing is simply that you interpret your own dream. The analyst or therapist hasn't dreamt your dream. You dreamt your dream. If the interpretation isn't mainly yours to as great an extent as possible, there will be an inherent level of distance and abstraction that complicates deeper understanding.

If you're aware of and accept that all dreams are instructive, the process in itself becomes an incentive to work harder. It's not only fun, fascinating, and exciting but also potentially essential when seen in relation to the survival instinct. In this "cosmic ultraholism" you, as the dreamer, communicate with an overall and permanent life force or intelligence through your own active filter (being a synthesis of concepts like human being, individual, sleeping environment, cerebral and emotional processes).

There are good reasons why dreams often use symbols or aestheticized seed in these instructive displays. The pioneering intuitions of

Freud and the early psychologists were correct: the two waking thirds are based on programmed behavior and a hierarchic structure. It's a simplified way of thinking and a simplified communication that's based on nuance-less causality. Here, only straight messages work, and if one message contradicts another, the vaguer or weaker of the two will give way, even if you know on a deeper and more emotionally resonant level that that option was actually the right one. This is why there is another kind of language in the dream sphere.

We can extract this level of "anotherness" to an esoteric sphere of various human exploits in history, not seldom focused on extraordinary inner experiences: occult science, initiatory rituals and teachings of fraternal organizations, magical societies, individual psychonauts, and so on. Human symbolic worlds have been consciously created (or translated from the dream sphere) to bring a certain knowledge or tradition onward in as pure a form as possible. That is, as untainted as possible by vague and causal human language, which also has a tendency to change with time.

The hypnopompic state (that is, when you drift out of sleep and into waking) is generally more difficult to control mentally than the hypnagogic (that is, when you drift from the waking state and into sleep). The reason is of course the feeling of pleasant well-being that sleeping means to most of us, and the enormous attraction of the dreams themselves.

Another way of increasing both recall and a general contact with the dream sphere is to express it in an artistic form. This doesn't mean that the method can only be used by artists but that you use methods that are suitable to give form to what you've dreamt and your own interpretation of that. The dream notebook could be seen as the most primitive example, but an interpretive text can lead to more. It's the same for drawing or painting—the recreation of the dream sequence in images. The reason is, as mentioned before, twofold: you get a better reflection surface for concrete interpretation and you thereby value the process as such.

In one's own interpretation of the dream lies also the possibility of changing the perspective. Consider that the dream you have experienced and remembered perhaps wasn't dreamt by you at all but that it is something that was presented for you from the outside, like an existential gift.

To give an outer form or shape to something inner is classical magic. To give form to something desired through artistic work like poetry, drawings, paintings, sculptures, or whatnot is to awaken life within the desire. That goes for nightmares too, although hopefully the other way around: the expression creates a catharsis of the undesired. The creative externalization of dreams apparently has therapeutic qualities of many kinds; this has been integrated in some segments or schools of psychology in different forms of art therapy.

The question is if it stops there, if it only stays at this "phase one," meaning that it's liberating to see what you've dreamt in a new way. I would like to argue that both frequency and intensity in this process increase the dream-sphere contact interface in itself. Recall becomes easier, which facilitates more efficient interpretation work. It also brings an increase of general existential stimulation in the form of fascination and joy, which I absolutely ascribe to the literally essential function of dreaming. An analogy: you can eat various kinds of junk food under stressed circumstances or you can consciously eat good and nutritious food under relaxed circumstances. What you choose will affect life as a whole, not only the alimentary system and its work as a purely physiological phenomenon.

We often appear in our own dreams. This indicates not only a personal presence in a kind of poetic flow of irrational wishes but can just as well indicate an instructive process. What you experience in the dream is meant for you and no one else. The identity and recognition of one's own presence is a language that activates receptivity for messages from the dream sphere.

Under normal circumstances we awaken with and in dream fragments, fascinating and attractive for sure, but they fade so quickly in that we often unwillingly approach the waking state. We are quite often so stressed already here that we don't even have the time to treat the frustration concerning the evanescence of the dreams. But do the dreams still linger on somewhere inside us? Are all dreams stored like our sensory impressions, in an enormous dream bank? If dreams aren't just loose fragments of memories but, as I argue, very concrete and individualized transmissions from much higher frequency levels, then perhaps it's possible to improve one's reception and simply receive more? The ether is full of an enormous amount of frequencies and messages that our senses cannot register, but they're still there: radio, television, wireless Internet, telecommunications, spy signals, and many other things. In that sphere, it's a question of adapting existing technology to be able to receive what is relevant to the communication in question. Our receiving technology when it comes to the dream sphere is the brain, and it can definitely be trimmed and calibrated to receive and interpret more. A lot more.

As often in life when it comes to mind-expanding or potentially life-changing experiences, modern individuals have a hard time taking their own experiences seriously enough to allow them to become concrete and meaningful parts of a life in creative flux. In the dream sphere, it becomes doubly problematic: we are raised in a culture in which this sphere is not given a high priority, yet the word itself indicates many ideal forms for us—dream girl, dream boy, dream team, dream scenario, and so on. And we're all on very deep levels endlessly fascinated by the attraction of the dreams but generally powerless in approaching them. We also live like slaves in the digital dictatorship of entertainment, in which we're swamped by symbols and dreamlike films and images. This is something I perceive as distinctly weakening our own dreaming.

It's not unusual that creative people have a good and active relationship to their own dreams, regardless of how concretely they work with them. We shouldn't just mention the strict, sleep-based dreaming here but also active imagination, daydreaming, hypnagogic states, hypnopompic states, and deep forms of meditation. Again, this is not only for or by artists. Many scientists, engineers, philosophers, writers, and others who live by thinking in new ways often feel a kinship with the attraction to the abnormal within dreaming. On a general level though, these people are exceptions rather than rules.

But it hasn't always been like that. Even in the West, dreams used to be more integrated. During antiquity, Greek physicians often consulted dreams in their diagnostic and healing work. Plutarch's stories of antique Greek and Roman lives are filled with integrated dreams, on religious as well as personal planes. A lot of people probably associate this systematic or prioritized dreaming with so-called primitive cultures, as is the case with magic in general. A big difference between then and now is that dreaming used to be collectively integrated in almost all the world. Today we dream alone. Well, at least in our cultural sphere. In Tibetan scholastic Buddhism advanced dreamwork is integrated in meditations and other forms of inner work, with basically the same goal as for everything else that is striven for: to see through the dream mechanisms and try to leave these and everything else behind in an enlightened state of nirvana.

Mark Twain and many other inspired authors have claimed that telepathy is completely normal and that the dream sphere is that place in consciousness where you can travel freely as you will, even in time. All that's needed is basically that you (a) value the process, and (b) start working with it.

The engineer Edison was close to addicted to his hypnagogic moments, as he learned early on that his best ideas came while in hypnagogic states of mind. After having worked in a very high tempo mentally he usually allowed himself what he called catnaps. He sat in his office chair with two steel balls, one in each hand, then drifted off. When he fell asleep properly the balls fell to the floor and the sound woke him up. Very often he had a new idea clear in his mind then.

Quite often these eureka moments come after an intense intellectual work process that the person in question then sets free in a dream sphere. Einstein had been thinking about his theory of relativity for ten years, and when his epiphanic moment eventually arrived, it arrived after a dream that drifted into a hypnopompic state. Here we can see an analogy to traditional magical thinking, in which a work of will culminates in a ritual, after which you set the desired effect or result free to find its own manifestation where and when it's suitable.

Goethe, Wagner, Brahms, Puccini, and hundreds if not thousands of other prominent artists of different kinds have all admitted their debt to either dreaming proper or hypnagogic states of mind.

Kekulé, the man who discovered the benzene molecule in 1890, did this in a revealing dream in which a snakelike being moved around in a, to Kekulé, molecularly applicable way. The facts were already inside his rational intellect but he needed to have that final detail presented to him under irrational circumstances. It's interesting how these key moments are never spelled out, so to speak, but always come in a symbolic form that makes the lock unlock. It seems as if the symbolic world of images is richer and often more efficient that rational clarity.

Art history is of course filled with people who've created remarkable things, and I think most of you know this sphere better than that of benzene molecules. We have to mention the surrealists, who not only jumped out of dreams in terms of inspiration but also to a great extent externalized the dreams in their artworks. This may have increased their personal dream contacts. But they also helped to undermine the conservative, destructive, and postindustrial consciousness of the Western world. The strong and often erotic surreal images and texts, to a great extent inspired by Freud and psychology in general, created a higher level of tolerance of "inner spheres" and "dream languages."

A more contemporary example would be David Lynch, whose

surrealistic inspiration, and that stemming from his own transcendental meditation and his own dreams, has contributed to so many masterpieces. When Audrey Horne in *Twin Peaks* starts dancing at the diner and says "Isn't this music dreamy?" it becomes a little piece of a mosaic of a new use of language. When something is strange, eerie, irrational, and dreamlike, we say today that it's a "Twin Peaks moment" rather than using a stricter reference to a dream atmosphere.

It can indeed be dream promoting to be exposed to other people's dreams and their creative externalizations of them. You get rid of some negative rationality under controlled circumstances in a cultivated comfort zone. But the effect will be much greater when you actively start working on and with your own dream sphere.

Let us now finally toy with the idea that what we do during our two waking thirds is simply to move the biological being onward. We add nutrition and work for survival and at the same time get really tired, all of this simply to make possible and optimize the most important third of our lives—that of sleeping and dreaming.

Some of us are more or less individuated and we feel a harmony in our lives and work. How can that be? Isn't it possible that it has to do with an optimal placement of individual capacity in a greater totality of a life-affirming movement? Aren't we all actually receiving information about these things in the instructional moments of our dreams? Is the basic problem simply that a weak recall obstructs an increased awareness about our own capacity and our own existential potential? I would absolutely say so.

Summing up then:

- Dream recall is possible to extend by an increased valuing of dreams by immediate notes, interpretations, and artistic externalizations.
- It's extremely important that the interpretation of the dreams is your own.

- Consciously prioritized dreamwork in general brings increased dream response (frequency, strength, resonance).
- The dream sphere is not only made up of fragments of memories or wishes that the brain as a neurological composite tries to process to recreate "order" during sleep. Dreams are not exclusively irrational expressions of subconscious desires.
- The dream sphere is beyond time and space and outside causal, logical (that is, man-made) structures.
- The dream sphere contains directed individual messages containing information and advice in regard to behavior on individual and collective levels. A simple analogy is ether-based media and wireless Internet, where you have a sender and a receiver, and which requires a specific technology.

18

Collective Mysticism

It's Probably a Myth

Originally a lecture delivered at the
Babalonium Gathering, Skåne, Sweden, 2014.

WHEN WE BEGIN TO LOOK at the term *mysticism,* which we can allow ourselves to use for the lack of a better one, we soon realize it is probably the most important thing there is within this exciting area of research we work in. There are many entry points and motivations to begin with some kind of esoteric self-development process, but it's often the same kinds that become truly decisive. In the "inner"—regardless of where we wish to place that sphere—things, emotions, information, and advice appear that can be life changing. The methods may vary: meditation, ritual, chemo-gnosis, sex, conscious exhaustion, and so on. In mind frames where our rational police force is temporarily short-circuited, things, symbols, intelligences, spirits, and beings quite often pop up. Some may be ephemeral or just entertaining, whereas others may tangibly affect us and the rest of our lives. It is almost like we're containing a large amount of relevant truths and insights but that we're fearful of taking part in it all. Why? Because it would considerably affect the controlled rational reality of daily life.

Mysticism exists in all cultures, all religions, all esoteric societies. The experience and its insights may then be clothed in cultural or religious clothing, but it's always a highly personal phenomenon. Most cultures early on indoctrinate against this kind of experience and call it unreal or evil or devoid of meaning. Now we're talking about power structures, that is, collective defense mechanisms of organisms and processes. If someone within a given collective randomly experiences or allows him- or herself to experience different and overwhelming things on the inside, free and without assistance from established and sanctioned professional proxies, there might be a chance that others would want that too, which could complicate things enormously.

We're living in a culture where most of the inner experiences are rationalized away as hocus-pocus. We don't risk death or too heavy stratification if we explore these things, but a sense of ridicule and stigmatization is totally possible if you don't adapt and conform to the comfort-zone control.

What this is really all about is taking oneself seriously. This is very important. You have to take yourself seriously. You have to take your impulses seriously and interpret them through your own, individual filter. Even within specialized esoteric systems there are equally hindering and stigmatizing functions that contain the very same ingredients as outside: structures and power. And then there is the mighty prerogative of interpretation. The aspect of interpretation becomes especially difficult as having overwhelming experiences in the inner is something most people actually *want* to share with like-minded people. But within all structures and hierarchies there's the risk that you demote yourself at the cost of someone else's validation or interpretation. This is very counterproductive.

It could be that collective systems in general, despite meaning well, actually oppose the individual flow of inspiration, thoughts, and ideas. I'll say "could be," as I have no evidence of it. And the reason for this is simple: I don't want any evidence of it, nor of the opposite. And the reason for this is even simpler: I value my own flow and my own source, so to speak, higher than many other things in life. In my own interpretation model it simply doesn't work to apply "mine" to "yours" or vice versa.

Now we're getting closer to the core of the dilemma. Could it be that there is something distinctly un-Thelemic—even within the Thelemic magical "system"—that in the outer consists of a distinct power structure with interpretation prerogatives, and that also contains techniques that try to integrate empiricism in something that basically consists of single epiphanies in an ultrasubjective and highly irrational individuation process?

Is it at all possible to methodically work to achieve epiphanic states of mind? I'm sure it is, but it's far too easy to be drowned in a "systematism" or in repeated, rational hopes as self-fulfilling prophecies. What works for one doesn't necessarily work for another. Yes, there may be a collective unconscious à la Jung, and maybe we all essentially experience the same mythical symbols in a certain state of mind that can then also be shared. And yes, there may be intelligences and beings that pop up like dogs when you call them by their right names, over and over. And yes—who knows?—there may even be cosmic forces that need our help as individual human beings, and vice versa. But the question remains whether all of these techniques and collective perspectives in totality signify a devaluation of the decidedly individual principle of intuition.

The mystical experience can probably only be validated through the effect it has in the moment or in the process of integration. Does it affect life? Its directions? Does it linger? We can see many parallel things within the dream sphere. We all know that dreams are amazing and we are inspired by them, terrified by them, we enjoy them and respect them. But yet they're not fully there when we wake up, that is, wake up to the benevolent tyranny of the rational mind. Epiphanies and reception of esoteric energy and information take place in a different state of mind that is not a dream state. And even here there is the usual devaluation of the value itself, even with those who've actually experienced it all: "It was just a weird thought or perhaps it was a daydream. No matter what, it wasn't for real. . . ."

But this doesn't really concern us here, because we belong to those who take this seriously. Yet new and critical thought processes always occur. It is as if the rational at every cost must protect normality and its power structures. Yes, perhaps it was a revolutionary personal insight but still it needs to be validated through a specific magical system to be able to be sanctioned as being "real" or "relevant."

It is the safety functions of the collective environment that have developed rationality and so-called normality. Its tool is a language that's usable for one sphere but not for the other. It's enough to communicate basic information and emotions but not in deeper (or higher) composites or clusters. Instead, art, poetry, music, and other creative expressions have been responsible for that important interface function throughout the millennia.

One of the main critical arguments against language, for instance in Buddhism, is the tendency to not be able to avoid the fact that it inherently contains one subject and one object; there is an inherent structural dividing line between seer and the seen. If language isn't enough it is of course incredibly difficult to convey something outside the causal and the already known. As D. T. Suzuki put it,

We cling to language and think that it is the thing which it represents. This habit of taking the symbol for reality does a great deal of harm in our daily life. Language is a most useful instrument, perhaps the most important means of communication that we humans have ever invented, but we frequently fail to understand that because of this usefulness, language enslaves us.[1]

To listen to a stoned individual eventually becomes quite depressing, regardless how amazing everything seems to be for the person in question. In the case of Eastern philosophy, the platitudes can become almost ridiculous: "All is one," "All is love," and so on. Perhaps all is one, but what does that really mean? And how can you integrate an insight like that without becoming like a noncritical member of a cultic egregore? Of course you have to experience it yourself to be able to understand and interpret. Perhaps you choose to formulate it in a similar way, and perhaps not.

The human being has a fundamental need to share both inner and outer experiences with others, not infrequently to claim territory and strengthen his or her position of experience. But the sharing can also take place because of genuine altruism or because one simply can't help oneself. When the need to share becomes stronger than the ability to empathically feel if someone is interested in listening or not, complications occur. But the sociopathic comedy (or tragedy) that can take place at moments like that doesn't necessarily mean that the original personal experience is without value or meaning. The challenge lies in the language one uses, and when.

Let's take a look at Crowley's elaborate system and well-known slogan, "The method of science, the aim of religion." The method of science? This basically means repeated experiments—so-called empiricism. But why should a single experience that will never come back (despite repeated attempts with the very same technique or ritual) be devoid of meaning or value? Why should its effect be looked down upon? Why should the technique or the prerequisites be looked down upon simply because they can't be perfectly repeated? To strive for a rational exactitude and analysis of things that belong on completely different planes is, in my opinion, to repeatedly hit your head against a wall of dull and painful concrete.

The method of science? Perhaps. The risk of spiritual imperialism becomes a tangible threat. The aim of religion? Perhaps.

The risk of fanaticism and fundamentalism becomes an equally tangible threat.

Good ideas never need to be tested empirically unless the *application* of the idea within a certain environment demands it. Usually ideas get a life of their own as soon as they've reached the surface. And all ideas are definitely not utilitarian; that is, they're not there to be used systematically and rationally at all. If you encounter an intelligence or different kind of being in a higher state of consciousness, isn't it then a bit condescending (or even rude) to come back after this and ask for the same answer or the same insight *again*? There must surely be a risk that the intelligence or being in question will end up believing that you are mentally challenged. But if you take that unique epiphany seriously, things could indeed get interesting.

Many scientists, both well-known and not so well-known, are as conscious of the mysteries of the origin of ideas as mystics or artists. It's always a question of a eureka moment—a distinct leap of progress, a quantum step, a caprice, a flash—despite the fact that the daily grind may consist of methodical, trench-digging, empirical work. It is the mind frame of the immediate moment that facilitates the growth and blossoming stemming from a seed that may have existed underneath the surface for a long time. One of our most brilliant scientists during the twentieth century, Nikola Tesla, wrote a lot about his own creative processes. It's fascinating when an extremely rational individual and scientist accounts for the details:

Back in the deep recesses of the brain was the solution, but I couldn't yet give it outward expression. One afternoon, which is ever present in my recollection, I was enjoying a walk with my friend in the City Park and reciting poetry. At that age I knew entire books by heart, word for word. One of these was Goethe's *Faust*. The sun was just setting and reminded me of the glorious passage:

The glow retreats, done is the day of toil;
It yonder hastes, new fields of life exploring;
Ah, that no wing can lift me from the soil,
Upon its track to follow, follow soaring!

A glorious dream! though now the glories fade.
Alas! the wings that lift the mind no aid
Of wings to lift the body can bequeath me.

As I uttered these inspiring words the idea came like a flash of lightning and in an instant the truth was revealed. I drew with a stick on the sand the diagrams shown six years later in my address before the American Institute of Electrical Engineers, and my companion understood them perfectly.[2]

I believe that the key to this is simply that you immediately take your own experiences and impressions seriously. An impression isn't worth more or less because it is diligently being analyzed by a rational mind frame. Safety is an illusion. Conviction always contains the seeds of fanaticism. Messianism is a romantic relationship to the denial of solipsism, where you take for granted that someone else cares as much as you do. Quite often it is a misdirected hope.

Each and everyone's truth is unique, just like in the cases with the central terms *will* and *love*. As far as I know, will can't be rationally analyzed. "If will stops and asks Why, invoking Because, then Will stops & does nought / If Power asks why, then is Power weakness," and so on.[3] The same for love, unless you break down the term itself and its emotional cluster into strictly biochemical particles. But that isn't really something one does, is it?

Structures always mean safety in authority. This is something most people need on some level. But valuable realizations usually come when you actually break the norms, structures, authorities, and safeties—at the least one's own. It's not exactly like an end in itself, but almost. Let's not forget that the health of a structure or organism is also kept up and vital by allowing a certain degree of rebellion. If that isn't allowed, the immune defense system can't strengthen the totality, which eventually could be fatal.

Paradoxically, we live in a culture that doesn't fully encourage irrationality and intuition via usable, essential techniques but still happily provides them via demagogic proxies like fiction and entertainment. Rational and critical processes are dulled by passive reception of irrational signals and mind-numbing programs. That which is supposed to facilitate communication and an exchange of information usually leads to the opposite. Today, we're learning through fiction rather than through fact, and this via technical platforms rather than intuition, curiosity, and inherited wisdom. Even here we can see an interesting and dynamic sphere between the individualistic and collective perspective. It's not the technology or the scientific triumphs that constitute the problem in itself. On the contrary; these are excellent for individual learning and inspiration. The problem lies in the collective and commercial application of the technology. And in the latter, there's usually an integrated set of morals that undermines individual initiatives and the individual's reliance on his or her own intuitive motion. This perspective thereby reminds one of the relationship between the subjective, esoteric process of individuation and existing systems, structures, and groups. The possibilities for revolutionary personal change are within reach, but they are drowned in prepackaged solutions that, of course, are sold for a hefty fee.

But "different strokes for different folks." In the valuing of one's own path there must always be a tolerance in regard to others. No matter how crazy or absurd other people's paths may seem, there simply are no templates that are applicable for everyone. But when you're genuinely on your own path you're not supposed to have either time or energy enough to criticize others. It's a fact as certain as the one that shows that the frequency of auspicious synchronicities increases when you're on the right path—that is, your own path.

Is there then no evidence in favor of a more homogenous and collectivistic view? The one closest to hand is scientific, in the sense of "biologistic." If we are equipped with filtering and defense mechanisms that are the same for all of us as a species, then the direct, gnostic, epiphanic experience and its physical, biological prerequisites could be too.

One symbol within Hinduism and later on within psychedelic mythology is the third eye—the eye that facilitates inner visions and insights. On a purely aesthetic-mythological level, the eye of Shiva has been a perfect symbol for the human desire to see more. But in actual fact there's more behind this than meets the eye (even the eye of Shiva!). The third eye has been isolated and defined as the pineal gland, which is situated between the brain halves in the front side of the brain, as a kind of bridge. This gland is actually the remnant of an actual third eye. One living example of (and possible evidence for) this theory is a New Zealand lizard, the tuatara, that has a section at the middle top of its head with a third eye inside it. This parietal eye is no longer connected to the sight center of the brain but has started to function as a gland. Already in the nineteenth century a conclusion was made that our own pineal glands had at one time been exactly like this.

The hormone that is secreted from this gland in mammals is called melatonin. We recognize the name from the little pill you take when you're jet-lagged and trying to normalize the sleep cycle (which of course regulates the dream cycle). Melatonin is created in the gland after having been triggered by serotonin: the agent or substance that sends nerve impulses via the synapses. Humans have more serotonin than other mammals, and this has led to advanced, abstracted thinking and creative impulses, making it a highly significant key to our own evolution. If we posit that the gland was actually an eye once upon a time, or existed as an even stronger gland with higher levels of serotonin, it is highly likely that early humans experienced much stronger visions. It can't be ruled out that a higher dose of melatonin from the pineal gland affected sleeping in a much more dream-inducing way. We should also add here that psychedelic agents like mescaline and LSD are highly releated to serotonin. LSD is basically a "serotonin blocker," but it's in the cerebral chaos when the serotonin again creates synaptic "order" that we have the psychedelic experience and all of what that brings. The consumption of alcohol effectively blocks production of melatonin. Consumption of cannabis increases it.

The third eye within us is a real, scientifically proven gland and function that is on the one hand followed by synaptic speed (a prerequisite of all cerebral activity) and on the other hand connected to visionary states of mind. Its mythological status as an all-seeing, inner eye is thereby not purely fiction but rather a preserved Ur-memory.

There has also been research done into the relationship between the pineal gland and sexuality. There seems to be a tight connection between them. A reduced function of the gland leads to both larger genital organs and a stronger sex drive. This could indicate that visionary tribes and cultures had less sex and therefore dwindled, and perhaps also that an increased sex drive and the contemporary insane level of breeding is a contributing cause to a poorer visionary culture on a global level.

One beautiful myth within Buddhism is the one in which the Buddha reached enlightenment under the famous Bodhi tree. The enlightenment came via sensory impressions, as he, according to the myth, was looking at the Morning Star, the planet Venus (later on associated with Lucifer), and that the brightness of the star, and the eye and brain in conjunction, brought him to an illuminated state of mind and an ensuing superconsciousness. For detail's sake, we should add that the fruit of the Bodhi tree (*Ficus religiosa*) has the highest level of serotonin of all fruits on this planet.

All the great mystics who have left substantial traces behind have consistently preached a direct, personal contact with the higher (or deeper). These ecstatic moments themselves may have been violent or peaceful, but what unites these mystics is a kind of self-imposed distance that defies the norms of their times. They have intuitively felt that the time is ripe for something new and they have followed that intuition until the illumination appeared. The collective structures that followed suit have all been defined by their own contemporary needs and expressions, for good and bad, but that still doesn't cloud the essence of pivotal personal moments and mystical impressions that, if the individual takes them seriously, will contribute constructively to the multifaceted mosaic called life.

Despite the fact that everything may eventually just be a big cosmic joke or an illusion, I still believe it's worth taking seriously. That's why I'll say good-bye with a hope that your third eyes will now reawaken to new, enthusiastic, and flirty life.

19

Challenging Inertia and Entropy

Originally a lecture delivered at the OTO Croatia
Conference in Split, Croatia, 2014.

WE KNOW, or at least assume with certainty, that everything is in flux, movement, motion. Our senses and interpretations provide us with this data, as does our immediate memory. We also have a tendency to ascribe cyclical directions to the movements in question. Energies revolve and life force is exactly that: a revolving force that helps or initiates further movement. On very tangible levels most of us have seen, heard of, or perhaps experienced that death means exactly the opposite: a lack of force and thereby movement. And when that process sets in, new energies are immediately set in motion to decompose the formerly so-alive vehicle or body. So in a sense, there's no real stasis even in death.

In the history and mythology of magic, terms like *energy* and *direction* have always been essential. It seems that extroverted and directed energy, set in motion by will, is *the* common denominator in all systems, schools, and traditions. Even mystical systems, schools, and traditions are involved in the very same thing; the only difference being that the direction of the energy has been changed, going inward instead of outward into the cosmos.

Can we then simplify and say that magic is (*a*) a knowledge of the energies in question, and (*b*) a harnessing of these so that they can be directed as willed? I think so. Most of what we can see in the history of magic is schematically the same. There may be different names and motivations and degrees of complexity, but we're still talking about consciously willed use of what already exists within and around us.

But what happens when routine sets in? Lack of motivation and will? When a formerly effective ritual turns into a dutiful ceremony? When a formerly pleasing situation turns into mere run-of-the-mill diluted experience? When an organism merely exists, apparently without meaning?

Here's where and when we encounter the terms *entropy* and *inertia*. They always set in sooner or later, perhaps as a necessary movement of decay before an actual decomposition, or, if we're lucky, as an eye-opener and instigator for change. When we are alive and somewhat conscious, we can make decisions about the direction of the energies. That's a beautiful trademark of what it means to be a human being. But still, far too many humans accept defeat, decay, and decomposition far too easily, although it's not at all necessary.

Entropy is a word that comes from thermodynamics and means, in simplified terms, energy that is isolated, unconnected, nonmoving. Following the second law of thermodynamics, the entropy of an isolated system always increases. This is not exactly the same as stasis, in which everything is still, but signifies energy that is contained and thereby not creating heat anymore.

Inertia is also a term borrowed from classical physics and, again simplified, means that a thing continues in its motion and direction, in a kind of unwillingness to change—or an inability to change.

Many people suffer from entropic states as well as from states of inertia, and sometimes these can be found in combination, for instance, in someone who is self-contained and therefore just keeps moving in the same direction. This situation might just as well be called a lonely force of habit. And of course, this phenomenon can also exist in groups or societies.

One way of angstfully repressing an approaching state of inertia and entropy is by positional rigidity, meaning that the person in question sticks with what was once meaningful and valuable to him or her, and gradually devalues everything else. This process can be seen in any kind of fundamentalism, as the views and perspectives become more and more narrow in the glorification of the safe haven that perhaps once provided a necessary fuel for a continual personal development.

Any kind of fundamentalism is always a sign of inertia and entropy on the individual level. On the larger scale, though, active mindlessness and active obedience from the, for instance, religious or political parts can greatly vitalize the larger group, entity, or even state. But it's still fed by elements of individual inertia and entropy.

I believe that the individual has the power to change things, and that collectives are essentially void of power unless there is one individual perspective that is commonly or communally backed up. That said, an individual could then potentially change an entire collective or organization suffering from inertia and entropy. But, sadly, that is more of an exception than a rule.

When do inertia and entropy set in? I'm sure a million answers could be given, but one of the most relevant could be "When the will to change on one's own terms becomes subservient to personal comfort, relying on ideals and systems based on other people's authority and inherent responsibility."

So how does creativity fit into this puzzle? Well, it's not as simple as saying that all you have to do to break a force of habit is start painting or write a poem. That can surely be therapeutic for some but also constitutes a kind of escapism if you're not really inclined to paint or write.

Everything begins with an idea and all ideas come from somewhere. Regardless of whether it's immediate solutions to everyday problems, big inspirational waves, or the big bang of a holy guardian angel encounter, the blooming of an idea is probably the most joyful and potentially habit-breaking phenomenon we experience in life.

If we allow ourselves to generalize, we can say that there are four main instigating moments:

1. Stillness, as we know it in meditation or hypnagogic states.
2. Sidetracking or diversion, as we know it from those moments when we look for something forgotten and temporarily leave that frustrated train of thought.
3. Transgression, which is a more forceful variant of number 2, and means being aware of something that lacks an idea and yet working on something completely different, for instance something diametrical.
4. The third mind; for example, in conversation and troubleshooting with others, the creative feedback generated and shared can make unforeseen ideas manifest, as if a third creative party or mind were present.

It seems that ideas are not very likely to appear when pulled, but rather want to push themselves, which is quite a beautiful symbol. This is elegantly conceptualized in Taoism by the method or attitude of *wu wei,* confusingly translated as "doing by not doing." This means basically working away at something but not overzealously or with too big a pulling effort; in a way, it's not attaching too great a rational energy to whatever needs doing. The resulting pleasant work mode is today usually called a flow.

Both inertia and entropy are hard nuts to crack. One requires a nudge or perhaps a smack and the other a break of isolation. It seems then that number 3, transgression, would be the most appropriate method for both. Not only is it challenging to do something that is not "you"; doing so most definitely sets things free within you. It's a chaos generator, if you will. This in no way means that you should go against your will for the sake of it, but rather look at it as a technique that makes you more aware of what your will actually consists of. Because true will is never embedded in inertia or a static position. It changes along the years, just like your physical organism-vehicle does. There is a light that never goes out, of course, a center of your universe, but it's very important to keep questioning yourself and your motives in the process. Because the processes of yesteryear are not the same as the present ones. If you cling dogmatically to what was once magical, you are likely to suffer from inertia and an entropic state of mind, which, in a worst-case scenario, can bring dogmatism or fundamentalism.

Originally, I had in mind to *not* mention Crowley or Thelema at all in this lecture. That in itself was quite a huge challenge. Perhaps it's a form of entropy to always have to rely on good old Uncle Al in Thelemic settings. In a way, I believe that's actually true. However, when we're on this subject there is such a brilliant example of the attitude I've touched upon in one of Crowley's greatest and most entertaining texts. I'm referring to an essay in *Konx Om Pax* with possibly the greatest title ever: "The Synagogue of Satan."[1]

Basically, the text is a humourous display of practical advice based on what we can call diametrical dynamics, meaning that if you're prone to or compulsive in one kind of behavior, you need to at least try the exact opposite in order to break any kind of entropic or stagnant state of mind, or lifestyle. Put another way, the goal is to eventually unite the opposites, energized by the transcending or transgressive movement.

The real title of the piece is "Thien Tao." It is interesting that this philosophical treatise hints at Taoism, as does the text in itself in many ways. *Konx Om Pax* was first published in 1907, eleven years before Crowley's major Taoistic enlightenment on Esopus Island on the Hudson River that was so overwhelming that he, the very logos of loghorrea, couldn't express what he had experienced properly— probably for the first and last time of his life. But there was a reason for the Taoist presence. The year before, in 1906, Crowley had spent time in China and was well acquainted with both the *Tao Te Ching* and other Chinese classics.

The story is very simple: A sage, Kwaw, as in Kwaw Lee, we can assume, gives good advice to a comfort-zone-inclined ruler. Everyone in his ruling classes is recommended to go in an opposite direction for two months each year.

> There are men who make a fetish of cleanliness; they shall work in a fitter's shop, and learn that dirt is the mark of honourable toil. There are those whose lives are rendered wretched by the fear of infection; they see bacteria of the deadliest sort in all things but the actual solutions of carbolic acid and mercuric chloride with which they hysterically combat their invisible foemen; such would I send to live in the bazaar at Delhi, where they shall haply learn that dirt makes little difference after all. There are slow men who need a few months' experience of the hustle of the stockyards; there are businessmen in a hurry, and they shall travel in Central Asia to acquire the art of repose.[2]

Crowley wrote that the text "gives my solution to the main ethical and philosophical problems of humanity with a description of the general method of emancipating oneself from the obsession of one's own ideas." This is pretty radical I think, for a Crowley post–*Liber AL* reception but prior to any major *Liber AL* analyses. And it ties in pretty well with what I've touched upon, namely that any situation, moment, or phase will turn to inertia and entropy if not eventually challenged and kept in motion, so to speak. The force of habit is enormous in the human psyche, and the greatest compensation for all ills and weaknesses is seeking comfort. I'm not saying everyone has to go completely crazy from time to time and oppose their own wills—that's absolutely *not* the point—but sometimes it's better to give oneself an active wake-up call than to receive it from someone or something else.

So how does creativity help in all of this? Does everyone need to try his or her hand at painting, like Crowley actually did? Of course not. I'm not saying that art in itself is the key to this. But creativity is. No matter which field you work and perhaps occasionally get stuck in, being creative is always an option. This means sometimes taking some time off, standing back, looking at things from a new perspective, "outside of the box," as people say nowadays. In a mind frame completely diametrical to what you're used to, new things appear. These things and insights can then be applied to your normal life and work. That's being creative.

An artist is used to being inside associative mind frames and intuitive flows. But that does not in any way imply a perfect mental health or balance. Even artists or traditionally creative people can be victims of inertia and entropy. They often are. They should allow a new method that is rational, strict, divided, stratified, and so on, to see what comes out of that. Perhaps nothing at all. But the mere jolt of looking at the world with new glasses should bring plenty of insights to integrate into one's own creative process.

Most of us, even devoted magicians, are stressed human-being ants, going from here to there and often forgetting to stop at times and evaluate. The contemporary human being needs a huge dose of stillness and quietude to be able to even focus a thought or two. And focus, we should always keep in mind, is not the same as singlemindedness. Meditation and yoga are invaluable in this regard, as is sleep of course. And being in nature, where chi is flowing freely.

The stillness and silence most of us desperately need should of course not be confused with either inertia or entropy. Balance never means passivity. Although the physical system may temporarily shut down, the inner meditations may drift in active flights of fancy. Or, if the meditation is actually totally still, deeper strata will be activated and leak messages and ideas to the higher strata. This could be called an ultra-creative state. As mentioned before, everything we create in any field of life stems from ideas, and ideas come from somewhere. When you find that link, use it well.

You can't force ideas to appear. If you can, you're probably too advanced for us here. Even in the magical process there is an analogy to this. Once the seed of will has been sown in ritual, it's always best to focus on something compelety different, to let it bloom in peace. Great ideas usually pop up like flowers when you're not thinking about the problem or challenge in question. It's almost as if it's a force that needs to be rerouted to appear. It should push itself from the inside and out, and not be pulled from outside.

If there are signs of fundamentalism or demagogic stagnancy in someone or something, you can rest assured it's a matter of inertia and/or entropy. If no one or nothing challenges this, sooner or later a crisis point will emerge, in which a kind of death occurs and decomposition sets in. My suggested remedy, as from Crowley and many others, is simply to stay aware of these mechanisms and keep them at bay with continual personal challenges. Of course, the same attitude should be encouraged in group dynamics too.

All of this sounds simple. But in real life it is very hard indeed to not succumb to the already known and comfortable. The more we think about that, the more painful it usually becomes.

It's wrong to be specific on a personal level when it comes to other people. "Every man and woman is a star," and so forth. Pointing the finger at someone else is usually a blunt camouflage of one's own inadequacies. The same goes for groups of people. If there are no challenges within the group structure to develop on an individual level, one should cock a very critical eye toward possible ulterior collectivisms, which are always un-Thelemic by definition.

There is a lovely book called *The Tao of Art* by Ben Willis that I can strongly recommend for those who are interested in these dusty and abstract topics. I would like to end this talk by quoting from that book. It sort of sums it up, and even hints at our own cherished proto-mysteries. That is, if mysteries can actually belong to one specific entity:

Every act of true creativity is the utilization of Tao energy and of the Tao nature which is inherent in the intuitive mind and foundational being of man. Indeed, such creativity is indistinguishable from that spiritual mind and from the Tao, for they are one, and of the same substance and nature. The creative force is the energy and flow of life—it is life itself.[3]

20

Memes or Schemes

Originally a lecture delivered at the Occult Humanities Conference, New York City, United States, 2016.

THIS WONDERFUL CONFERENCE is very symptomatic of the times we're in.* One thing leads to another, and people's appetite for phenomena and expressions beyond the merely causal and rational seems insatiable. But are we looking at a meme, that is, a small or large contagious building block in a large construction of a potential future, or a scheme, that is, a conscious strategy that has already been willed? That is something I will humbly address today.

The occult is a romantic and fascinating part of our cultural history. It has also been the breeding ground for ideas and concepts that have later on been integrated in the natural sciences, religion, and psychology. The occult is also a cluster of promises containing a small, valuable signal of transformation at the center of an enormous nebula of symbol-induced noise and psychological compensation. If not impossible, then at least one could say it's very difficult just to say what *it* is. However, as a keyword or catchphrase in contemporary culture, we have seen it take more and more place both within fiction and fact.

---

*An exhibition of occult-themed artworks called "Language of the Birds" was on display at the 80WSE Gallery parallel to the conference, which was held at New York University from February 5–7, 2016.

Pop culture has been heavily immersed in occult and fantastic themes of various kinds, via Hollywood and TV, in literature, and in music for more than a decade. Exactly parallel to that, academic interest in predominantly Western esotericism has boomed, with relevant chairs appearing at universities almost yearly. Ditto within the sphere of art, where the fantastic, mythological, spiritual, and intuitive is more and more visible on a larger and larger scale. And the sphere itself, that is, magic and occultism as a mix of philosophy and behavioral techniques, some traditional and some entirely new, is also on the increase via the Internet on one hand and beautiful publishing of both old and new works on the other. There is no longer a heavy stigma, and there's certainly no shortage of information for those who are interested in these fascinating areas of human existence.

It's not so strange that a phenomenon such as this occurs, that is, has a presence in culture. That has happened many times before, often during liberal and humanistic phases of cultural mutation, although often also heavily stratified and moderated by general attitudes of religions and morals. Usually, it's the artists of different kinds who have carried the seed of human potential and expressed whatever they have found, either to enthusiastic freethinkers or antagonistic conservatives. Today, it seems to be a different ball game altogether. We live in an era that is saturated and amplified in every possible way, but most of all via popular media and social media.

How do we look at this? Is it a genuine liberalization and so-called democratization via the mere availability? Or is it a conspiratorial strategy to flood both the Web and the market with things to keep the masses pacified and confused? One way of looking at it could be to use the concept of a meme. The term was originally coined by evolutionary biologist and anti-religionist Richard Dawkins as signifying a cultural counterpart to the gene, the smallest building block of life, in constant flux, development, and possible mutation to attempt maximum survival. Dawkins's comparison is not bad at all. Because more than ever, we are no longer mere biological creatures causally striving to avoid the eventual certainty of life, which is death. We are cultural human beings immersed in a flow of information, views, sentiments, and reactivity. In this lies the possibility of choice, especially within cultural spheres that allow individual choice. If I understand Dawkins correctly, a meme is then a seed of sorts, a protoconcept that can be either symbolic or literal, but that instigates actual change when it is integrated in a larger context by contagion.

As most of the larger contexts are willed, that is, defined by one or more human beings as having a chosen direction, we can call these schemes. One needs the other: a meme only becomes tangibly potent within a scheme, an environment of reception, interpretation, and integration. Schemes need willed concepts, originating as simple memes (ideas, notions, frustrations, key terms). The point where the meme is integrated into or transformed into a scheme is one of transcendence that sets energy free. For example, sniffing a perfume of someone loved that is missed can bring forth an evocative presence, releasing well-being; or simplistic political sloganeering can lead to a particular outcome in an election. They seem to belong together, in the same way a gene and a chromosome does, or a chromosome and a human existence. Or a human existence and greater culture as such.

Social media has great potential to mislead, confuse, and obfuscate, not only through the conscious strategies of lobbyists and organizations but also through good old-fashioned human error. A funny and recent example here in the United States was a call to solidarity in regard to the Powerball $1.3 billion jackpot. Someone created a meme/post encouraging the winner to share, based on a calculation that with 300 million American citizens, everyone could get $4.33 million and poverty would be eradicated immediately. More than a million people immediately shared the original and very altruistic post without thinking. The only problem was one of miscalculation: with the sum and the amount of people, each citizen would actually get $4.33, which today unfortunately is not enough to eradicate poverty. But it certainly showed a contemporary behavioral pattern that is very eager to share an opinion—even though it's objectively a wrong one—and a sentiment in great numbers. The meme turned into a seemingly benevolent scheme that then became a new meme—this time of unfortunate scorn.

The borders between fact and fiction are increasingly blurred these days. I have stated before that fiction is the new fact and has superseded traditional ways of learning, which leads to great uncertainties in terms of quality control, academic standards, and values. In our fantastic little occult corner of culture, which we can call the suprarational and truth seeking, we can be amazed at not only the *potential* mutations but also marvel at the already existing hybrids. An example: Some of us remember the *X-Files* from the nineties, a TV series integrating not only UFO-related mysteries but also a lot of occultism and paranormal phenomena. It was total pop, yes, but still highly entertaining and interesting, specifically considering creator and producer Chris Carter's questioning of nontransparent governmental organizations. This led to both pro and contra conspiracies: the TV series was, on the one hand, flaunting an attitude based in and on individual rights and a wider possibility of strange phenomena, many of which could be labeled occult. On the other hand, it was criticized by more radical elements as *being* a conspiracy in itself, a smokescreen to divert serious attention from covert activities. Recently, as I'm sure many of you know, a brand new season of the series has emerged. The first episodes were even harsher in their criticism of governmental conspiracies than the original ones, which were pre 9/11. The CIA has now almost humorously responded by making available UFO and other material from their archives, presenting them as their X-Files and making references to the *fictional* characters of FBI agents Mulder and Scully: "Mulder would have loved to get his hands on this." This blurring between fact and fiction and interexchange of memes (within possible schemes) has never been as manifest as now. Entertaining, yes. But from a conspiratorial point of view, it's dangerous. If people consume more fiction and readily accept memes on social media without criticism, then the field is literally open to modify the memes as the controllers see fit—which is basically the same as what's going on in the empire of genetic research.

In the midst of quite heavy entertainment on occult themes, whether inspiring or conspiratorial, there lingers still a slight sense of ridicule, which in itself could be both another smokescreen or a safeguard for inspiration turning into substance. If we consider the *American Horror Story* season called *Coven*, the existence for the teen heroine witch can't be easy, as she kills the men she has sex with. That symbol of a young vaginal two-edged sword is both potentially repressive and liberating, and the mere existence of it within mainstream TV I find remarkable. At the same time, the common media phenomenon of teen witches usually calls these women "twitches." Sure, a slightly humorous play on words, but also a term signifying quite blatantly a nervous disorder symptom.

From the literally occult or gnostic meme-versus-scheme perspective, there is what I would call an advantage. Chris Carter's slogan "The truth is out there" or Agent Mulder's "I want to believe," or even Agent Scully's "I want to *dis*believe," all reflect a causal, rational, sensory-based approach based on empiricism. The gnostic memetic schemer knows that the truth is already "in here" and that it's not possible to *want* to believe: one either does or doesn't. This accepting vantage point can indeed be amplified by empirical research *if* one so desires, but it's only interesting from a schematic point of view: that is, if you have something to sell—philosophy, a method, a book, a workshop, and so on. But it's certainly not necessary. There were many reasons why occultism as such was kept stigmatized and hidden in varying degrees over the millennia. But one factor rarely addressed was simply that this kind of work is personal, individual, intuitive—gnostic, by definition. The more systematized and objective something becomes, the greater the risk of it becoming part of psychosocial circuses, petty power struggles, and essentially non-altruistic schemes. However, the creative possibilities of the opposite always remain: whenever a meme morphs into a scheme, it becomes transdimensional, sets energy free, and thereby becomes inherently magical.

In the exhibition *The Language of the Birds* we can see examples of interpretations and expressions based on individual filtering of non-rational, nonintellectual stimuli. Whether these come from within, from without, or from beyond is quite irrelevant. The artworks affect us in varying degrees based on deep resonances. This is of course valid for non-occult art too. Something in a specific artwork makes us stop, feel, reflect, and integrate. It is a language in itself based on the emotional or sentient rather than the intellectual, mental, or word based. But the distinctly occult art acknowledges the power of myth and symbol for what it is: an absolutely essential ingredient of life and the individuation process. Reconnecting with a primordial sphere via aestheticized expressions is not only personally liberating but also *possibly* healing for others.

Things always seem to emerge in culture for which there is a need. On the more general level, superheroes in fiction always seem to appear when there is an abounding sense of powerlessness and fatigue. Antigovernment conspiracies appear when the gap is simply too big between citizens and rulership. LSD appeared at about the same time as the atomic bomb was developed and unleashed. Vaccines are developed when an epi- or pandemic is threatening. And the occult literally pops up when the normal, scientific explanations become too abstract, distant, redundant, or elite. Art and entertainment reflect, yes, but always also contain new memes, quite often beyond the comprehension of even their creators, and quite often very vital in their seeking new hosts to mutate.

If we look back at human civilization, what remains to be analyzed and evaluated are basically the works of art. Writings and artworks tell a story of not only what people did but also what they felt and how they looked at their own world. This has proven to be invaluable in understanding human development. In the future, the analysts of our times won't be let off so easily. Not only will there be more concrete stuff in the rubble: mountain ranges of technological waste, organic-plastic hybrids at sea, and urban wastelands to penetrate, but any evidence of written history will most likely be nonexistent because of data evaporation. And contemporary art, if someone will be able to find it, will mostly be abstract on many levels: either as strictly formal and thereby redundant, or as needing an intellectual explanation, such as an interpretation or instruction manual.

Artworks that contain a pure intuitive filtering and expression—no matter how formally competent or incompetent—have the ability to convey sentiments and messages to the future. Not infrequently, we can see that these artists also share a similar subconscious approach to life in general: a susceptibility to intuitive survival modes beyond the personal ego. Even in the bleakest dystopian visions lie seed or memes of great potential change. Even in the most shallow New Age pastels can be found diamondlike facet spectra, filtering indestructible light and energy. I think one key to *relevant* art is that it doesn't present prefab solutions but rather distinctly resonating surfaces for further individual introspection. It encourages speculation. The same I think is true of the cluster we call occultism. What we see on the surface we can either regard or disregard. But if we shut down the defense systems temporarily, we can allow an influx of life stemming from another mind, whether contemporary or ancient. Memes that are eventually integrated don't lose potency, but sometimes they do need to be looked at in a new context. The genetic comparison is again quite useful. We are not only now. We have already existed, through our genetic history, for a long time and will hopefully continue. Perhaps not in exactly the same kind of human form, but still. . . . The truth is in here.

The lure of occultism shares many traits with other human idealized "isms." One is the romantic notion that there are hidden masters working for improvement via initiating structures, with colorful teachers disseminating specific teaching in order to cultivate the ennobled individual. This is no different from a university, a military organization, a religious organization, a political movement, or an artistic institution. The schematic analysis is basically the same. But occultism differs slightly in regard to what is contained: an active refinement of the *inner* spheres rather than the outer. And with suggested techniques that have not yet been accepted as science by the contemporary definitions or standards. That said, one could argue that contemporary occultism is no longer about performing arcane rituals using traditional elemental or planetary symbols but rather about experimental art, cognitive psychology, neurology, and applied physics—preferably all of these in union. This is what's now considered as potentially liberating, in the sense of "empowering," and thereby also potentially threatening to the pacifying forces, similar to the way Kabbalah, tarot, meditation, and yoga were looked down upon not that long ago.

Another different trait or quality is that the memes received in so-called occult theory and practice don't need outer recognition to be validated. What's received and integrated comes from deeper or hidden aspects of oneself, and the only relevant validating force is the individual him- or herself. To be able to do that, one needs to be a stable and secure individuated human being. Solid internal memes should be the building blocks within distinctly individual schemes. The Delphic motto of *Nosce te ipsum* ("Know thyself!") has never been more relevant than in our era of massive and simplified homogenization. In this sense, occultism can also become a romanticized trap, offering endless possibilities of escapism, compensation, and counterproductive self-aggrandizement. It's not enough to know yourself: you also have to assume responsibility for what you find. Otherwise the memes you discover or codify may not match any greater schemes at all.

Is there an actual equation or a relationship here? That is, is the allure of the potential scheme tied to the incapacity of the partaker obsessed by the memes themselves—as I actually perceive many occultists to be? Does it fulfill an escapist, compensatory function rather than a tangible, transforming one? With no further likenesses intended, perhaps we could look at the difference between athletes and sports fans; the inspiring memes of sports and fiercely brave competition attract those who long for physical, existential change in their own life schemes that perhaps seem impotent or just comfortably complacent, but how many actually transform the original memes into tangible, life-improving schemes?

The current magical revival in popular culture is in many ways symptomatic of a Western malaise and frustration with the given options, in which the individual is placed within either a materialistic collective or a reactionary monotheistic religion, or possibly a combination. Both are mere substitutes for a genuine existential worth and meaning that can only come from within, defined through active individuation. My theory is that the solutions are always a lot closer than we think. In regard to global environmental problems, it can certainly be tempting to long for outer space. But perhaps it's more intelligent to look around on our own fine planet instead, at cultures who have actually managed to survive through crises in history, either via still-existing, living indigenous humans or through remaining works of art. If we can assimilate instead of just "exoticize," we will find that there are many distinct traits in common, such as, for instance, a validation of inner, intuitive processes of gathering information, and a holistic approach to their implementation. This is beyond religion, occultism, philosophy, or magic. It's just common sense, in which memes from inner nature become schemes in outer nature, and possibly vice versa. I wouldn't be surprised if it's all essentially the same thing and that a free-flowing circulation will help mutate existence to ensure maximum survival, both on memetic and genetic levels.

In recent years, I've suggested exchanging terminologies between the traditionally occult and the traditionally artistic, thereby helping the assimilation of potentially transformative techniques and attitudes by discarding the arcane and often incomprehensible symbolic world in favor of a protocreative, perhaps even undefined, rationale of sympathetic behavior and strategy. A new generation of "artists of the soul" would need no formal training within either pseudoreligious groups or so-called art schools. It's all a matter of integrating an inner process of self-knowledge, desire, and, let's not forget, will, within an outer process of communicating the findings or results in a literally enchanting form, not just containing a willed expression but rather an expressed will. To paraphrase Dawkins's "selfish gene," I hope that artists will develop more selfish memes, in the sense of art ingrained with personal intention. With that perspective in mind, I think it's clear to see that our culture contains almost unlimited possibilities of self-expression and communication. For those curious and brave, it's no longer a question of memes *or* schemes, but rather one of a natural, intuitive merging of the two into a creative synthesis that transcends philosophy, art, literature, the occult, and so on, in jolts of further inspiration and advancement.

21

Intuition as a State of Grace

Originally a lecture delivered at Overgaden in Copenhagen, Denmark, 2014.

IMAGINE A PERSON fiercely focused on the creation of an object. He or she is undisturbed, and the surroundings are optimized for this specific creation. The vision is clear, sketches or preparatory fragments have helped the gearing up for the moment of execution, amplified by suitable music and perhaps even special clothes for the occasion. The tension increases, the work is begun, and when it's over, a great sense of well-being and release becomes overwhelming.

Did I just describe an artist or a magician at work? Did I just describe someone externalizing inner creative concepts or someone programming the cosmos? Well, both of course, as they're essentially the same in method and approach. This little talk today will focus on the conceptual similarities of the creative process involved in art and magic. As we'll see, there are considerably more aspects that unite them than set them apart.

This is not implying that the one always perfectly corresponds to the other. But there is more than enough common ground to see that the creative process involved is highly similar. What makes the two

220

areas differ is usually one of purpose and potential-in-extension.

The common ground is not surprising. At one point in time, art and magic were basically the same, intertwined and necessary for tribal well-being. Cave paintings, ritual dances, evocative music, programmatic poetry, talismanic jewelry, charged weapons were all part of a creative process with a distinct purpose: to make something desired happen and to make something undesired not happen.

As with many things in human cultural development, major existential shifts took place and things became specialized and compartmentalized—a process still going on today, for good or bad. The mystically spiritual and ecstatic became organized in religions with professional proxy-priesthoods. The previously integrated artistic expressions as agents of willed change instead became particular professions for individuals with a specific talent. But where did this talent originally come from?

In our human progress, evolution, and development, we contain everything that's passed before us in our DNA. We are like cosmic tape recorders in an ever-evolving process of refinement and adaptation. Special qualities needed for survival are passed on in tradition, myth, and genetic mass. This is still being conceptualized and expressed by artistically creative people in many fields. That's their function, so to speak: to move everything onward and bring the good stuff along.

As mentioned before, this creative strain was divided into specialized skills and professions. Some became scientists, some historians, and some continued manifesting their own personal visions in externalized artistic forms. These have been some of the main sanctioned expressions and professions within human culture. But there have also been those who've retained a traditional yet highly experimental labor in working with the unseen and immeasurable. Sometimes these have been more or less integrated in society, but most often not. The magicians have most often worked on their own or in small groups of like-minded souls. Dealing with basically the same behavioral methods and questions but usually with an added ingredient: personal will—meaning that what is created also carries a charge that helps change things in unseen, immeasurable, and presently unknown ways.

When art as such became integrated as a more or less necessary but commodified field of work, it was still an expression of this same human need. We need art and culture as reflective surfaces, personal catharsis, and release, as something to initiate existential conversations and thought fodder—essential fuel for progress and development. Everyone knows that, and it's always there. The amount of people actively dealing with art (as opposed to dealing *in* art) is minimal today compared to the totality of human beings, and yet the status is still high—that is, if the artist in question is successful. Even in the most totalitarian of societies, there is art to amplify the condoned, allowed, and encouraged agenda.

One should perhaps also enter the very sensitive question here: What exactly is art? There have been so many definitions over the centuries that one gets tired by the mere overview: Berenson's life-enhancement angle; Tolstoy's egalitarian, almost antibeatific angle; Goethe's and later Steiner's spiritual angle; Beuys's social sculpture angle; Gurdjieff's objective angle; Duchamp's sardonically detached angle—it's all one big mess or mesh of contradicting yet eloquent theories and postulates. It's really no wonder that contemporary art theory is so ephemeral and elusive. Basically, the definitions seem to go intimately hand in hand with whatever tradition or school will soon be obsolete. The only common denominator that really seems to permeate all of them is art's original function: a magical one. But that aspect is seldom looked upon with admiring eyes by our civilization's defining minds.

What then of magic? It's almost as chaotic there but more muddled and often quite vile. I think Aleister Crowley came up with the best definition so far: "Magick is the science and art of causing change to occur in conformity with will." All other attempts seem quite futile compared to that.

Even in the most well-ordered and confined expressions the artist often feels a need to go beyond the formal norms and normal forms. Art history is packed with individual examples that have led themselves straight into Draconian measures because they felt some kind of need to. The same is the case in the history of science. The pioneers are seldom praised until the masses catch up. And then it's usually too late to enjoy it. The deviators, rebels, iconoclasts have always been able to sneak at least some degree of seed sowing into works of art otherwise condoned and integrated in a wholesome totality of a "greater good." This can vary from a new stylistic touch to an unseen piece of content, as in hidden symbols, or even conscious subversions of content or form, and so forth.

Basic psychology tells us that the artist needs to express him- or herself, almost compulsively, putting feelings, desires, skill, excellence, or even self-doubt in a form that touches people enough to cause them to react. The reaction becomes a validation not only of the process involved but also of course of the person and mind behind it all. When that's not there, the frustration of invisibility and poverty abounds. When it is there, on the other hand, a deep-rooted sense of bliss and meaning takes hold. This vulnerability of the individual supports a strong system of market and moral control, which is something artists have far too often adapted to.

For reasons having to do with traditional stigma or ostracism, the magician has up until recently been quite content with working in silence or in a hidden sphere. Let's not forget that the word *occult* means "hidden" in Latin. That, however, doesn't mean that magicians and occultists have been less susceptible to personal sensitivity, weakness, and ego compensation. It's quite often the contrary. But there's one thing that usually sets their work apart from that of the artists. It's the concept of defined will. A magician has a distinct sense of purpose, a (hopefully) well-thought-through plan and a goal for the work in question. If it's a matter of a ceremony, it's to uphold a balance and atmosphere. If it's an active ritual, it's to change something specific in the small or grand arena of life. The creative process then acts as a means and not an end in itself.

It's interesting to note that magicians usually avoid the limelight, as the work itself holds precedence. The artist, on the other hand, can use both negative and positive visibility to his or her own benefit. That's simply because our society needs scandalous individuals and outsiders in general to relieve collective tension. A successful and media-conscious artist works equally well as a movie star. At times, magicians appear who take on celebrity or notoriety status, but they can only expect flack or negative exposure. Aleister Crowley and Anton LaVey are two well-known examples from the twentieth century.

So what unites these two protohuman endeavors that were once wholly intertwined? Some principal ties are:

- Irrationality as key or necessary agent. The rational mind frame hampers genuine creativity.
- Imagination and visionary ability. You trust what you perceive and not what others tell you to perceive.
- Heavy emotional engagement in the creative process (as opposed to purely causal, detached labor). If you don't feel and believe in what's going on, everything will be a barren and soulless endeavor.
- Externalization of inner processes. New life comes from within and moves outside.
- Creation as an umbrella for a supra-ecstatic flow: more than mere "joy" in working. Elevated states of mind, ideas, and epiphanies as results of the mind being in neutral gear, so to speak.
- Manifestation as building block or aggregate of experience. "A life's work." One thing leads to another, and if one is conscious of and grateful about it, many life-enhancing synchronicities will follow.

- Integration of the symbolic. Naturalism is not possible and only pleases the rational mind. Where schooling within a tradition is often necessary, the development of one's own language or code is crucial for maximum impact. In magic, this means, for instance, being schooled in one specific tradition like Western ceremonial magic and then drifting off into your own devices and methods. In art it could be schooling or being inspired within, for instance, surrealism, and then moving on in personal integrations of, for instance, scientific symbols and codes.
- An integrated breach of the previous stage: tradition is transcended, not seldom aggressively. Rebels rebel in both instances. Hiccups and revolutions are necessary for overall health because the most radical and extreme occurrences always end up as rigid and conservative environments. Iconoclastic bowel movements.

There is also another common key ingredient in this magical art-soup: intuition—that lovely nonrational flow of existence so cherished by Taoists and creative people. What exactly is it? It's a temporary freedom from causal bonds and rational thinking that sets inner creativity and happiness free. It's a well-known but pretty undefined positive state of mind that helps us a lot in decision making and creation. What would art be if intuition weren't there? A mere outer construction work of ideas or concepts. What would magic be without intuition? A mere reading of a cosmic user's manual. Trusting one's intuition may be the most important ingredient there is. Especially so in an overall culture that is increasingly binary and dualistic in both outlook and method.

An artist in our sphere of the world usually works in a much more causal and commodified structure than a magician. In your studio, you create. That's highly satisfying, but you also know that you have to get by by going through many motions to secure sustenance and exposure of your creations. That's because our culture as such only really allows "approved" entrepreneurs and manufacturers of acceptable influx through complex systems of exhibition, appraisal, validation, criticism, and financial compensation. If you play the game by the rules you're more than welcome to compete for your place in the sun of recognition and appreciation.

This is, of course, a generalized view of the situation, but no less true. Most artists unnecessarily restrain themselves by adapting to a very clearly defined set of rules. You fight and get bitter and disillusioned if you don't succeed, or fight and get happy if you do. In a way, the outer circumstances dictate the inner feelings because there's an outer arbiter or commander commenting and judging whether or not what you make has any value or merit as such.

But the direction should be from the inside outward. Yes, a filtering of external influx is inevitable and perhaps even essential. But it needs to be filtered on the inside, in the alchemical oven, in the fire, in the womb. Seeds come from the outside in, but the new life comes from the inside outward. That sexual or procreative analogy is a central one in both art and magic. Or should be. We should remember these kinds of very basic wisdoms from many bright minds within philosophy and magic, but perhaps specifically Buckminster Fuller when he declared: "Mimic nature and you can't go wrong!"

Let's zoom back to earlier phases when art was still ingrained with magic and vice versa. That is, when it had the power to change and not only entertain. When the power of the artwork, object, or performance wasn't measured by transactions validating the creator in question but rather by whether the outcome of its charge was successful. The worth of the artist then lay in the ability to systematize and charge chosen artistic expressions, like a sculpture, dance, song, painting, and so on. Success in that sphere guaranteed an elevated status within the tribe or commune.

In my experience, however, it's as if contemporary magic and its practitioners are lost in a maze of conservative content and very rigid traditional approaches to form when it comes to applying this ancient, primordial science and art to a modern world. It's similar to the way art as such has been pushed back to being an aestheticized, commodified world of forms filtered through desperate and petty egos and their external commanders, with too much content and energy on the one hand and too much form and intellectual nervousness on the other. It seems both areas have become victims of our binary times, with rigidity and lack of courage as banners. The result is that positions become heavier and heavier in the choking illusion of safety, with occasional volcanic, psychic outbursts when the respective intellectual decompression chambers aren't working as they should. There should be a healthier balance.

It seems I can't deliver a lecture without returning to one of the most potent and beautiful metaphorical scenes ever in movie history: Mickey Mouse as the sorcerer's apprentice in Disney's *Fantasia*. In youthful enthusiasm yet ample laziness, Mickey uses magical tricks to make cleaning house simpler. This is to catastrophic results. But he learns his lesson well from the returning and very angry magician: one needs to know not only the tools of one's trade but also to be very clear in what one wants to achieve with these tools.

What if a young generation consciously connected the currently separated ends of the power cable of meta-programmatic content and alluringly suitable form? And what if they not only joined forces but actually joined the very life force itself? It's a very challenging thought and potentially a dangerous one.

During the past decade, a keen interest in esoteric protagonists, movements, and artists has seeped into the art world. We have, for instance, seen a revitalized appraisal of masters like Swedish painter Hilma af Klint. The exhibition that was at the Louisiana Museum (outside of Copenhagen) last year has been seen by over a million people all over Europe. That hardly sounds like an esoteric exhibition. In 2008, the Centre Pompidou in Paris housed an enormous exhibition called *Traces de Sacré* (Traces of the Sacred), which was an overwhelming celebration of art and the occult. The Venice Biennale of

2013 was packed with works of an occult nature, ranging from Lady Frieda Harris, the woman who painted Crowley's Thoth Tarot deck, Carl Jung's *Red Book,* Borges's imaginary beings, and on to Xul Solar's collages. There are, nowadays, academic symposia focusing on the intersection between art and occult history. The term *occulture* is now almost mainstream and indicates previously esoteric themes as having been accepted and "exotericized." Also, new generations of artists are reexpressing and integrating occult, religious, or spiritual themes in their own way, both in form and content. This could vary from using Goethe's color schemes, listening to inner voices, experimenting with higher states of consciousness, allowing experiences in nature to shape one's expressions via inclusion of distinctly occult iconography in images and other kinds of works. Quite simply, the colorful gray area between art and the occult is established and ever growing.

To a greater extent than ever before, young artists tend not to separate the process from the product, so to speak. The process can be magical, and the art object then becomes something that carries a charge beyond the merely esthetic or personally cathartic. In fact, in these times, an increasing number of artworks become talismans. They are the results of a consciously willed yet intuitive process, and they contain remnants not only of that process as a result but also energy that has been set in motion in a desired direction. Whether the partakers realize or know this is irrelevant. But that artists work with this kind of thinking and making is in fact highly relevant and healthy.

Where art for so long has touched upon attribute rather than on essence, there seems to be a shift going on in which the positions are being diametrically changed. The essential meaning becomes more important than that of the attribute of aesthetics and commercial value. This of course brings us back to primordial times when it was indeed more important that the artwork contained power than an attractive surface. When language gradually took over, rationality and structure followed suit. Yet the need for the primordial, magical expression has been there all along and now seems to finally resurface within its own perimeters.

This is without a doubt an effect of a too-rational culture gone overboard. In our desperation to survive as a species, let alone as individuals, different remedies are needed than the ones prescribed by a status quo complacency. This is an all-permeating and anxious movement in our present times. So it's hardly surprising that art shrugs off some superficiality and assumes the responsibility it once had. Art should not only inspire us to live more fully and think free thoughts and feel free emotions. It should also present solutions and alternatives beyond the many rationalistic, materialistic, binary fallacies we have already experienced or committed. But the beauty of it all is that this is not going to happen in dogmatic, intellectual ways or through an abstract, postmodernist discourse. It's going to be more direct, vibrant, alive, poetic, emotional, violent, and expressive. Although perhaps shaped in entirely new languages and codes, it won't be hard to interpret at all. It's going to be guided by intuition and survival instinct and not by faint references to previous "isms" or demagogic simplifications to alleviate bad Western consciences. Individual intuition may be that original state of grace so brutally shoved aside by monotheistic religion to pave the way for hubristic self-destruction. The art that catches this drift and integrates protohuman desire and behavior will become the talismanic art that will literally help save the world as we know it and love it.

Acknowledgments

Warm thanks for supporting my work are due Margareta Abrahamsson, Sofia Lindström-Abrahamsson, Jon Graham, everyone at Inner Traditions, Peder Byberg, Jack Stevenson, Lea Porsager, Bjarne Salling Pedersen, Peter Steffensen, Pam Grossman, Jesse Bransford, William Koch, Morbid Anatomy, Michael Moynihan and Annabel Lee Moynihan, Andrew M. McKenzie, Genesis Breyer P-Orridge, Gabriel McCaughry, Thomas Tibert, Alkistis Dimech, Peter Grey, Thorsten Soma, Jonas Plöger, Claus Laufenburg, Susanne Witzgall, Kerstin Stakemeier, Dariusz Misiuna, Katarzyna Drenda, Helena Malewska, Bartosz Samitowski, Krzysztof Azarewicz, Ania Orzech, Vera & Stojan Nikolich, Marko Štefan-Poljak, Andreas Kalliaridis, Fredrik Söderberg, Ida Månson, Elisabeth Punzi, Torben Hansen, Rasmus Hungnes, and Martin Palmer. Extra special thanks are due Vanessa Sinclair, to whom this book is lovingly dedicated.

Notes

1. CONTRA CONTRA MEANS PRO

1. Breton, "Manifesto of Surrealism," https://tcf.ua.edu/Classes/Jbutler/T340 /SurManifesto/ManifestoOfSurrealism.htm (accessed December 14, 2016).
2. Fowles, *The Aristos,* 116.

2. SPLENDOR SOLIS

1. Steiner, "What Is Anthroposophy?" 263.
2. Steiner, "What Is Anthroposophy?" 263.
3. Williams, *Turning to Nature in Germany,* 28.
4. Williams, *Turning to Nature in Germany,* 37.
5. Frazer, *The Golden Bough,* 623.
6. Goodrick-Clarke, *Black Sun,* 3.

3. ABSTRACTION MADE CONCRETE

1. A much-expanded version of the previous *Thee Psychick Bible: Thee Apocryphal Scriptures ov Genesis P-Orridge and the Third Mind ov Psychic TV,* ed. Joe Rapoza.

4. OVER THE MOON AND BACK AGAIN

1. Walker, "The Moon," 1881.
2. According to Lukas Feireiss in his brilliant *Memories of the Moon Age.*

3. "Stanley Kubrick Confesses to Faking the Moon Landings," www.youtube
.com/watch?v=rR4pf6pp1kQ. Excerpted from the film *Shooting Stanley
Kubrick* by Patrick Murray, 2015. The theory was earlier elaborated on by
Jay Weidner in the film *Room 237* (2012), about Kubrick's *The Shining* in
this excerpt: www.youtube.com/watch?v=_u4A5tJ2j3o. Also see the film
Dark Side of the Moon by William Karel (2002), and Bill Kaysing's book *We
Never Went to the Moon: America's Thirty Billion Dollar Swindle* (1976).
Websites accessed on October 1, 2016.

4. "How the Easter Date is determined," accessed October 1, 2016, www
.timeanddate.com/calendar/determining-easter-date.html.

5. Eisler, *Man into Wolf,* 19.

6. WHAT REMAINS FOR THE FUTURE?

1. Gerald Yorke interviewed by David Tibet in Yorke, *Aleister Crowley, The
Golden Dawn and Buddhism,* 208.

2. Steiner, "Goethe as the Founder of a New Science of Aesthetics," 61.

3. Steiner, *The New Essential Steiner,* 180, 187, 192.

4. Donne, from "Meditation 17," in *No Man Is an Island: A Selection of the
Prose of John Donne.*

5. Crowley, "Liber Thisharb," in *Book Four,* 648.

7. PAUL BOWLES

1. Miles, *William S. Burroughs: A Life,* 253.

2. Miles, *William S. Burroughs: A Life,* 253.

3. Miles, *William S. Burroughs: A Life,* 271.

4. Bowles, *Without Stopping,* 125.

5. Bowles, *The Sheltering Sky,* 14.

6. Bowles, *Without Stopping,* 116.

7. Maugham, *The Summing Up,* 27.

8. Maugham, *The Summing Up,* 184.

9. Brion Gysin in the foreword to his *Stories,* 5.

10. Bowles, *Without Stopping,* 366.

11. Paul Bowles interviewed by Simon Bischoff in *Paul Bowles: Photographs,* 254.

12. *Let It Come Down: The Life of Paul Bowles,* film directed by Jennifer
Baichwal, 1998.

8. TANGIBLE EVANESCENCE

1. Jünger, *On the Marble Cliffs*, 23.
2. Mishima, *Sun and Steel*, 72.
3. Mishima, *Sun and Steel*, 102.
4. Mishima, *Sun and Steel*, 57.
5. Jünger, *On the Marble Cliffs*, 69.
6. Mishima, *Sun and Steel*, 41.

9. ANTON LAVEY: MAGICAL INNOVATOR

1. LaVey, *Satanic Bible*, 155.
2. LaVey, *Satan Speaks*, 9.
3. LaVey, *The Devil's Notebook*, 133, 138.
4. LaVey, *The Satanic Rituals*, 11.
5. LaVey, *The Satanic Rituals*, 22.
6. LaVey, *The Devil's Notebook*, 78.
7. LaVey, *The Devil's Notebook*, 80.
8. LaVey, *The Devil's Notebook*, 17, 63
9. LaVey, *Satan Speaks*, 30.
10. LaVey, *Satan Speaks*, 22.
11. LaVey, *The Devil's Notebook*, 140.

10. CARL JUNG, MYTHMAKER

1. Jung, "The Psychology of the Child Archetype," 83–84.
2. Campbell, *Creative Mythology*, 637.
3. Eliade, *The Myth of the Eternal Return*, 34.
4. Jung, *Aion*, 269.

11. THE IMAGINATIVE LIBIDO

1. Marie-Louise von Franz, introduction to Hannah, *Encounters with the Soul: Active Imagination*, 2.
2. LaVey, "The Construction of Artificial Human Companions," 138.

12. FORMULATING THE DESIRED

1. Freud, "Dreams and the Occult," 108.

14. THE MEGA GOLEM IS ALIVE AND WELL

1. Meyrink, *The Golem*, 19.
2. Meyrink, *The Golem*, 44
3. Meyrink, *The Golem*, 71–72

15. SEXUAL-DYNAMIC POLARITY

1. Crowley, *Magic without Tears*, 63.
2. Crowley, *Little Essays towards Truth*, 89.
3. Wilhelm, *The Secret of the Golden Flower*, 24.
4. Crowley, *The Confessions of Aleister Crowley*, 714.
5. Leah Hirsig, quoted in Symonds, *The Great Beast*, 254.

17. THE MAGIC OF DREAMS MADE REAL

1. Roger Knudson, quoted in Moss, *The Secret History of Dreaming*, xxi.

18. COLLECTIVE MYSTICISM

1. Suzuki, *Field of Zen*, 50.
2. Tesla, *My Inventions*, 39–40.
3. Crowley, *Liber AL: The Book of the La*, 43.

19. CHALLENGING INERTIA AND ENTROPY

1. Crowley, *Konx Om Pax*.
2. Crowley, *Konx Om Pax*, 63.
3. Willis, *The Tao of Art*, 41.

Bibliography

Abrahamsson, Carl, ed. *The Fenris Wolf 1–3*. Stockholm: Edda Publishing, 2011.

———. *The Fenris Wolf 4*. Stockholm: Edda Publishing, 2011.

———. *The Fenris Wolf 6*. Stockholm: Edda Publishing, 2013.

———. *The Fenris Wolf 8*. Stockholm: Trapart Books, 2016.

Baichwal, Jennifer, dir. *Let It Come Down: The Life of Paul Bowles*. DVD. Canada, 1998.

Bougas, Nick, dir. *Speak of the Devil*. DVD. Burbank, Calif.: Wavelength Video, 1993.

Bowles, Paul. *Photographs*. New York: Scalo, 1994.

———. *The Sheltering Sky*. New York: Ecco, 1978.

———. *Without Stopping*. New York: Ecco/Harper, 1985.

Campbell, Joseph. *Creative Mythology: The Masks of God*. New York: Penguin, 1968.

Cavendish, Richard, ed. *Man, Myth and Magic. No. 55*. London: BPC Publishing, 1970.

Crowley, Aleister. *Book Four*. York Beach, Maine: Samuel Weiser, 1997.

———. *The Confessions of Aleister Crowley*. London: Routledge & Kegan Paul, 1979.

———. *Konx Om Pax*. Chicago: Teitan Press, 1990.

———. *Liber AL: The Book of the Law*. York Beach, Maine: Red Wheel/Weiser, 2004.

———. *Little Essays towards Truth*. Scottsdale, Ariz.: New Falcon, 1991.

———. *Magic without Tears*. St. Paul, Minn.: Llewellyn, 1973.

Devereux, George, ed. *Psychoanalysis and the Occult.* New York: International Universities Press, 1953.

Donne, John. *No Man Is an Island: A Selection of the Prose of John Donne.* London: The Folio Society, 1997.

Eisler, Robert. *Man Into Wolf: An Anthropological Interpretation of Sadism, Masochism and Lycanthropy.* Santa Barbara, Calif.: Ross-Erikson, 1977.

Eliade, Mircea. *The Myth of the Eternal Return.* Princeton: Princeton/Bollingen, 2005.

Feireiss, Lukas. *Memories of the Moon Age.* Leipzig: Spector Books, 2015.

Frazer, J. G. *The Golden Bough.* London: PaperMac, 1987.

Fowles, John. *The Aristos.* London: Pan Books, 1968.

Goodrick-Clarke, Nicholas. *Black Sun: Aryan Cults, Esoteric Nazism and the Politics of Identity.* New York: New York University Press, 2003.

Gysin, Brion. *Stories.* Oakland, Calif.: Inkblot, 1984.

Hannah, Barbara. *Encounters with the Soul: Active Imagination.* Boston: Sigo Press, 1981.

Jung, Carl. *Aion: Researches into the Phenomenology of the Self.* Princeton: Bollingen/Princeton, 1969.

———. *Essays on a Science of Mythology.* Princeton: Bollingen/Princeton, 1969.

Jünger, Ernst. *On the Marble Cliffs.* Translated by Stuart Hood. London: John Lehmann Ltd., 1947.

LaVey, Anton. *The Devil's Notebook.* Portland, Ore.: Feral House, 1992.

———. *Satan Speaks.* Venice, Calif.: Feral House, 1998.

———. *The Satanic Bible.* New York: Avon Books, 1969.

———. *The Satanic Rituals.* New York: Avon Books, 1972.

———. *The Satanic Witch.* Los Angeles: Feral House, 1989.

Maugham, W. Somerset. *The Summing Up.* London: Mandarin, 1990.

McDermott, Robert, ed. *The New Essential Steiner.* Great Barrington, Mass.: Lindisfarne Books, 2009.

Meyrink, Gustav. *The Golem.* Prague/San Francisco: Mudra, 1972.

Miles, Barry. *William S. Burroughs: A Life.* London: Weidenfeld & Nicolson, 2014.

Mishima, Yukio. *Sun and Steel.* Translated by John Bester. New York: Kodansha Intl, 2003.

Moss, Robert. *The Secret History of Dreaming.* Novato, Calif.: New World Library, 2009.

Steiner, Rudolf. *Art: An Introductory Reader*. Forest Row, UK: Sophia Books, 2003.

———. *The New Essential Steiner*. Edited and introduced with notes by Robert McDermott. Great Barrington, Mass.: Lindisfarne Books, 2009.

Suzuki, D. T. *Field of Zen*. New York: Harper & Row, 1970.

Symonds, John. *The Great Beast*. London: Panther Books, 1956.

Tesla, Nikola. *My Inventions*. New York: Penguin Classics, 2011.

Wilhelm, Richard, ed. and trans. *The Secret of the Golden Flower*. New York: Harvest, 1962.

Williams, John Alexander. *Turning to Nature in Germany: Hiking, Nudism and Conservation, 1900–1940*. Stanford, Calif.: Stanford University Press, 2007.

Willis, Ben. *The Tao of Art: The Inner Meaning of Chinese Art and Philosophy*. Lincoln, Neb.: Author's Guild Back In Print/iUniverse, 2000.

Yorke, Gerald. *Aleister Crowley, the Golden Dawn and Buddhism*. York Beach, Maine: The Teitan Press, 2011.

Index